I0130477

HEROES OF THE
UNITED NATIONS

The Gstaad Project | Gstaad Publications

HEROES OF THE UNITED NATIONS

MEN AND WOMEN WHO MADE
THE WORLD A BETTER PLACE

EDITED BY ANDREAS SANDRE VON WARBURG

ILLUSTRATED BY MATTHEW COUPER

Printed in the United States by the Gstaad Project
ISBN-13: 978-0615467108
ISBN-10: 0615467105
BISAC: Political Science / International Relations / Diplomacy

www.gstaadproject.com

To my mother and father
who taught me about the world

and to Angela King
whose passion and dedication
have left an indelible mark on my life

§ CONTENTS

Introduction 15

Dag Hammarskjöld
. A Renaissance Man 31
. The Convincing Force of Ideals 37
. Monsieur H 43
. Dag Hammarskjöld and the Relation
of Law to Politics 51

Angela E.V. King
. A Woman of the United Nations 71
. Much Remains To Be Done 77
. Women, Peace, and Posts – In United Nations
Peace Operations 83

Graça Machel
. A Children's Champion 105
. The Plight of Children 111

. Impact of Armed Conflicts on Children 125

Eleanor Roosevelt
. The First Lady of Human Rights..................................... 139
. The Struggle for Human Rights 153
. To the Women of the World 169
. She Saw Clearly; She Spoke Simply 173

Helvi Sipilä
. Finland's International Lady.. 183
. Power is thus also a force for good 189
. Changing Roles of Women in the
  Developing Regions of the World 197

Carlo Urbani
. It Was a Tricky Call.. 209
. A Drop of Water in the Desert...................................... 215
. How Carlo Saved my Life 221
. Heroes and Heroines of the War on SARS.................... 231

Sergio Vieira de Mello
. A World of Dignity 249
. Iraq: the United Nations
  is Here for the Long Haul... 271
. Mourning the Man, Honoring the Message................. 281
. A Unique Cocktail of
  Qualities and Identities 285

Nadia Younes
. The Egyptian Princess 301
. A Burning Sense Of Justice 307

. She Could Laugh Louder Than Anybody Else.............. 315

Annexes
. Charter of the United Nations 327
. Universal Declaration of Human Rights 373
. Convention on the Elimination of All
   Forms of Discrimination Against Women...................... 383

§ INTRODUCTION

On August 19, 2003, a terrorist truck-bomb wrecks the United Nations Headquarters in Baghdad, killing the Secretary-General's Special Representative for Iraq, Sergio Vieira de Mello, and 16 members of his team. A few years later, on December 11, 2007, another suicide bombing attack in Algiers, the capital city of Algeria, took the life of 17 UN employees, the second highest death toll in the history of the United Nations. A few months earlier, on April 17, 2007, a roadside bomb struck a UN convoy in the city of Kandahar in Afghanistan, killing five staff members.

And the death toll does not stop there. According to the United Nations Staff Union's Committee, in 2007 at least 42 UN staff members were killed on duty, making it one of the deadliest years ever for the Organization.

"This tragedy (...) is about a savage loss inflicted on the entire United Nations family," UN Secretary-General Ban Ki-moon said during a memorial ceremony for those who perished in the Algiers bombing. "From UNDP to UNIDO, from ILO to UNAIDS, from UNFPA to WFP and UNHCR – our colleagues worked at the United Nations in Algiers not to pursue a political mission, far less to promote the interests of one group of nations or peoples over those of another. They were there to work for development, support sustainable industrial growth and promote employment and training. They were there to fight AIDS, advance women's health and meet the needs of refugees. They were there to help build better lives for the men, women and children which the UN exists to serve."

But terrorism is not the only factor to take into consideration when working for the United Nations around the world: on January 12, 2010, a horrifying earthquake shook the capital of Haiti, in the Caribbean, killing 102 UN men and women including the Special Representative of the Secretary-General in the country and head of the United Nations Stabilization Mission in Haiti (MINUSTAH), Hédi Annabi. In the words of UN Secretary-General Ban Ki-moon, "Forty-seven seconds. It is not a long time. But the earthquake in Haiti was an eternity of sorrow."

Indeed, those men and women died for what they stood for. They died serving humanity's highest ideals. They died in their effort to make this world a better place for all.

Thousands of people are employed by the United Nations and other international organizations in the most dangerous spots around the world, where intestine wars, famine, drought, and natural disasters are killing millions of innocents every day. They are heroes who chose to spend most of their life in poor and under-developed countries in order to make a difference, to improve and save the lives of as many people as possible. They don't represent a country, they don't travel first class, they don't go to lavish diplomatic dinners and parties. Instead, they risk their own life for world peace and security, for providing food and clean water to the poorest people on Earth, for fostering gender equality and social justice, for promoting human rights.

Sergio Vieira de Mello was one of them, and possibly the best-known casualty of war for the UN family. Born in Brazil in 1948, he joined the United Nations at the age of 21 and spent most of his career working for the UN refugees agency – eventually becoming the head of the UN High Commissioner for Refugees in 2002 – and humanitarian and peacekeeping missions around the world. Before going to Iraq, he managed the political transition to the newly independent Timor-Leste (East Timor). In Iraq he lost his life, but not his fight against injustice and poverty.

Today, Sergio Vieira de Mello still inspires thousands of students and young graduates to join the United Nations, the Red Cross, the World Bank, the North Atlantic Treaty Organization and many other specialized, regional, and international institutions around the world. Indeed, risks are considerably high when working in dangerous areas – just as they are for any other international worker, such as war correspondents, military personnel, or private contractors.

But the reward is infinite: saving the life of just one person marks a big step forward for humanity. And that is what "world diplomats" do every day working behind the scenes.

Sometimes a diplomat may be "more of a soldier than a diplomat," as former UN Secretary-General Javier Perez de Cuellar describes one of his closest right hands, former chief UN hostage negotiator Giandomenico Picco. But what did de Cuellar mean by that? Just like Sergio Vieira de Mello, Picco spent most of his career in the United Nations system, before leaving the Organization in 1992 for the private sector. And just like Vieira de Mello, he risked his own life more than once for UN causes. As a UN high-ranking official, he put himself on the spot to ensure the release of Western hostages in Lebanon in the early 1990s. He disappeared from sight for several days and traveled countless times to intimidating Shiite strongholds in Syria and Lebanon. Only his assistant knew his whereabouts and even the Secretary-General was kept in the dark. He agreed to negotiated kidnappings of his own person in order to secretly meet with the captors; he was moving to a different location every night with a contract on his life. His mediation was successful, and the risks he took were fruitful.

"History does not kill," Picco writes in his memoirs.[*] "Religion does not rape women, the purity of blood does

---

[*] Picco, Giandomenico. Man Without a Gun. One Diplomat's Secret Struggle to Free the Hostages, Fight Terrorism, and End a War. New York: Times Books/Random House, 1999

not destroy buildings, and institutions do not fail. Only individuals do these things."

But individuals are also the custodians of peace and development cooperation traditions set by international institutions. And individuals are the backbone of these organizations – brave individuals that are fighting to save even one single life, in both under-developed and wealthy countries, at home and abroad.

Heroes of the United Nations: men and women who made the world a better place wants to honor all those individuals who – following the footsteps of Sergio Vieira de Mello and Giandomenico Picco – are striving to make a difference, all those courageous international civil servants who are working to end injustice and promote freedom.

Following are stories of behind-the-scene men and women. Brave and spirited people who dedicated their lives to helping others. Take for example Carlo Urbani, a WHO physician and infectious disease specialist whose work defined the Severe Acute Respiratory Syndrome, also known as SARS. Urbani died in Thailand on March 29, 2003, of SARS, leaving behind his wife and two sons; but also a powerful legacy, of devoutness and dedication. "Shortly before Dr. Urbani became ill, his wife worried about the danger in which he was putting himself," Lee Jong-wook, former Director-General of the World Health Organization, said in his eulogy. "Dr. Urbani replied: 'If I cannot work in such situations, what am I here for - answering emails and pushing paper?' Carlo Urbani has given us at WHO its best - not pushing paper, but pushing back the assault of poverty and disease."

Heroes of the United Nations is about people and for people. It's a way to honor the Organization and make all of us part of it. Sergio Vieira de Mello, Carlo Urbani, and Angela King were everyday people, just like us. They made the UN part of their life and transformed it into a vehicle of peace.

In his 2001 Nobel lecture, former Secretary-General Kofi Annan said: "This award belongs not just to me. I do not stand here alone. On behalf of all my colleagues in every part of the United Nations, in every corner of the globe, who have devoted their lives – and in many instances risked or given their lives in the cause of peace – I thank the Members of the Nobel Committee for this high honor. My own path to service at the United Nations was made possible by the sacrifice and commitment of my family and many friends from all continents – some of whom have passed away – who taught me and guided me. To them, I offer my most profound gratitude."

Following the twin truck-bombings in Algiers, and to confront the increasing security risks that the United Nations and its staff are facing around the world, Secretary-General Ban Ki-moon appointed a special panel to look into security risks, headed by UN veteran Lakhdar Brahimi.

"Our flag that used to be a protection is becoming now a target," Brahimi commented during a press conference in early 2008. "And I'm not sure whether we have really absorbed that reality and acted on it."

Brahimi – whose name is associated with one of the UN's most influential reports ever, the so-called Brahimi Report on peace operations, including dysfunctionalities of the organization, and particularly its inability to carry out its mission for lack of proper global intelligence capabilities – knows the risks of working under the UN flag. He was Special Representative of the Secretary-General in Afghanistan and Iraq, and witnessed the end of apartheid in South Africa and the deployment of a 20,000-strong UN-led multinational force in Haiti in the mid-Nineties.

"People question the independence of the United Nations", Brahimi said. "They say, 'It's taking sides.' A lot of people are – some rightly, some not rightly – angry with the United Nations."

Indeed, whether we are angry or not with the United Nations, we need to realize that the men and women working under the UN flag are trying to make a difference. And no matter what our stand is – whether or not we support the United Nations and its work around the world – we need to honor the courage of every UN people and help them make our world a better place for all.

First and foremost, we need to provide a safer world for them to operate. According to a 2011 report by the United

Nations, since the Baghdad bombing in 2003, incidents have been increasing. Over the past ten years, attacks against UN staff and humanitarian workers tripled. The report, entitled *To Stay and Deliver: Good practice for humanitarians in complex security environments*, commissioned by the UN Office for the Coordination of Humanitarian Affairs (OCHA), indicates that the last decade was in fact the worst on record for attacks on aid workers, with on average 100 serious attacks per year for the last seven years. Since 2005, there had been 180 major attacks on aid workers in Afghanistan, 150 in Sudan, and nearly 100 in Somalia, with many other situations posing great risk, as well.

"There are no places on earth where humanitarian organizations should not go or can not go," Jan Egeland, former United Nations Under-Secretary-General for Humanitarian Affairs, said as he introduced the study that he had co-authored. "Instead of asking what does it take to leave, we should ask what does it take to stay in Mazar-i-Sharif and other such places. Risk management means you adapt to the circumstances," added Egeland, currently the Director of the Norwegian Institute of International Affairs. "

Unfortunately, the United Nations and aid organizations have a long way to go before humanitarian workers will be able to operate in a safer environment. People like Sergio Vieira de Mello and Nadia Younes lost their life because they believed in the UN. They believed that, in order to make a difference, the Organization should have stayed in areas like Iraq, Afghanistan, and other war-thorn countries. Their courage is their legacy to all of us in order to make our world a better place for generations to come. A step at a time.

DAG HAMMARSKJÖLD

Matthew Cooper 2002

Dag Hammarskjöld

"Dag Hammarskjöld was an intellectual and a visionary in action. He made a new art of multilateral diplomacy as well as giving a fresh and dynamic dimension to inter-national service. He was a strong believer in the future and in the capacity of human beings to shape it for the better. In our very complex times, his thoughts, his example, and his achievements are both a resource and an inspiration."

— Brian Urquhart
Former U.N. Assistant Secretary-General

§ A RENAISSANCE MAN

By the Nobel Foundation[*]

Dag Hjalmar Agne Carl Hammarskjöld (July 29, 1905-September 18, 1961) was the youngest of four sons of Agnes (Almquist) Hammarskjöld and Hjalmar Hammarskjöld, prime minister of Sweden, member of the Hague Tribunal, governor of Uppland, chairman of the Board of the Nobel Foundation. In a brief piece written for a radio program in 1953, Dag Hammarskjöld spoke of the influence of his parents: "From generations of soldiers and government officials on my father's side I inherited a belief that no life was more satisfactory than one of selfless service to your country - or humanity. This service required a sacrifice of all personal interests, but likewise the courage to stand up unflinchingly for your convictions. From scholars and clergymen on my mother's side, I inherited a belief that, in the very radical sense of the Gospels, all men

[*] Courtesy of the Nobel Foundation.

were equals as children of God, and should be met and treated by us as our masters in God."

Dag Hammarskjöld was, by common consent, the outstanding student of his day at Uppsala University where he took his degree in 1925 in the humanities, with emphasis on linguistics, literature, and history. During these years he laid the basis for his command of English, French, and German and for his stylistic mastery of his native language in which he developed something of the artist's touch. He was capable of understanding the poetry of the German Hermann Hesse and of the American Emily Dickinson; of taking delight in painting, especially in the work of the French Impressionists; of discoursing on music, particularly on the compositions of Beethoven; and in later years, of participating in sophisticated dialogue on Christian theology. In athletics he was a competent performer in gymnastics, a strong skier, a mountaineer who served for some years as the president of the Swedish Alpinist club. In short, Hammarskjöld was a Renaissance man.

His main intellectual and professional interest for some years, however, was political economy. He took a second degree at Uppsala in economics, in 1928, a law degree in 1930, and a doctoral degree in economics in 1934. For one year, 1933, Hammarskjöld taught economics at the University of Stockholm. But both his own desire and his heritage led him to enter public service to which he devoted thirty-one years in Swedish financial affairs, Swedish foreign relations, and global international affairs. His success in his first position, that of secretary from 1930 to 1934 to a governmental commission on unemployment, brought him to the attention of the directors of the Bank of Sweden who made him the Bank's secretary in 1935. From 1936 to 1945, he held the post of undersecretary in the Ministry of Finance. From 1941 to 1948, thus overlapping the undersecretaryship by four years, he was placed at the head of the Bank of Sweden, the most influential financial structure in the country.

Hammarskjöld has been credited with having coined the term "planned economy". Along with his eldest brother, Bo, who was then undersecretary in the Ministry of Social Welfare, he drafted the legislation which opened the way to the creation of the present, so-called "welfare state. " In the latter part of this period, he drew attention as an international financial negotiator for his part in the discussions with Great Britain on the postwar economic reconstruction of Europe, in his reshaping of the twelve-year-old United States-Swedish trade agreement, in his participation in the talks which organized the Marshall Plan, and in his leadership on the Executive Committee of the Organization for European Economic Cooperation.

Hammarskjöld's connection with the Swedish Ministry of Foreign Affairs began in 1946 when he became its financial adviser. In 1949 he was named to an official post in the Foreign Ministry and in 1951 became the deputy foreign minister, with cabinet rank, although he continued to remain aloof from membership in any political party. In foreign affairs he continued a policy of international economic cooperation. A diplomatic feat of this period was the avoiding of Swedish commitment to the cooperative military venture of the North

Atlantic Treaty Organization while collaborating on the political level in the Council of Europe and on the economic level in the Organization of European Economic Cooperation.

Hammarskjöld represented Sweden as a delegate to the United Nations in 1949 and again from 1951 to 1953. Receiving fifty-seven votes out of sixty, Hammarskjöld was elected Secretary-General of the United Nations in 1953 for a five-year term and reelected in 1957. Before turning to the world problems awaiting him, he established a firm base of operations. For his Secretariat of 4,000 people, he drew up a set of regulations defining their responsibilities to the international organization of which they were a part and affirming their independence from narrowly conceived national interests.

In the six years after his first major victory of 1954-1955, when he personally negotiated the release of American soldiers captured by the Chinese in the Korean War, he was involved in struggles on three of the world's continents. He approached them through what he liked to call "preventive diplomacy" and while doing so sought to establish more independence and effectiveness in the post of Secretary-General itself.

In the Middle East his efforts to ease the situation in Palestine and to resolve its problems continued throughout his stay in office. During the Suez Canal crisis of 1956, he exercised his own personal diplomacy with the nations involved; worked with many others in the UN to get the UN to nullify the use of force by Israel, France, and Great Britain following Nasser's commandeering of the Canal; and under the UN's mandate, commissioned the United Nations Emergency Force (UNEF) - the first ever mobilized by an international organization. In 1958 he suggested to the Assembly a solution to the crises in Lebanon and Jordan and subsequently directed the establishment of the UN Observation Group in Lebanon and the UN Office in Jordan, bringing about the withdrawal of the American and British troops which had been sent there. In 1959 he sent a personal representative to Southeast Asia when Cambodia and Thailand broke off diplomatic relations, and another to Laos when problems arose there.

Out of these crises came procedures and tactics new to the UN - the use of the UNEF, employment of a UN "presence" in world trouble spots and a steadily growing tendency to make the Secretary-General the executive for operations for peace.

It was with these precedents established that the United Nations and Hammarskjöld took up the problems stemming from the new independence of various developing countries. The most dangerous of these, that of the newly liberated Congo, arose in July, 1960, when the new government there, faced with mutiny in its army, secession of its province of Katanga, and intervention of Belgian troops, asked the UN for help. The UN responded by sending a peace-keeping force, with Hammarskjöld in charge of operations.

When the situation deteriorated during the year that followed, Hammarskjöld had to deal with almost insuperable difficulties in the Congo and with criticism in the UN. A last crisis for him came in September, 1961, when, arriving in Leopoldville to discuss details of UN aid with the Congolese government, he learned that fighting had erupted between Katanga troops and the noncombatant forces of the UN. A few days later, in an effort to secure a cease-fire, he left by air for a personal conference with President Tshombe of Katanga. Sometime in the night of September 17-18, he and fifteen others aboard perished when their plane crashed near the border between Katanga and North Rhodesia.

After his death, the publication in 1963 of his "journal" entitled *Markings* revealed the inner man as few documents ever have. The entries in this manuscript, Hammarskjöld wrote in a covering letter to his literary executor, constitute " a sort of White Book concerning my negotiations with myself - and with God." There is a delicate irony in this use of the language of the diplomat. The entries themselves are spiritual truths given artistic form. *Markings* contains many references to death, perhaps none more explicit or significant than this portion from the opening entries, written when he was a young man:

> *Tomorrow we shall meet,*
> *Death and I -.*
> *And he shall thrust his sword*
> *Into one who is wide awake.*

§ THE CONVINCING FORCE OF IDEALS

By Rolf Edberg *

It is with infinite sadness that I have received, at the request of the administrators of the estate of Dag Hammarskjöld, the prize for the year 1961 awarded posthumously to a friend and fellow countryman.

How thankful I should be if I could present to you what he himself would have thought and said, were he standing here today.

Surely he would have seen it as symbolic to be called to

* Acceptance speech by Rolf Edberg, Swedish Ambassador to Norway, on the occasion of the award of the Nobel Peace Prize in Oslo, December 10, 1961. Ambassador Edberg, representing the Hammarskjöld family, accepted the Peace Prize for 1961 awarded posthumously to Dag Hammarskjöld. The English translation of his speech is, with some editorial emendations, basically that appearing in *Les Prix Nobel en 1961*, which also carries the original Swedish text. Courtesy of the Nobel Foundation.

this stage - where so much human goodwill has been honoured - along with the South African advocate of nonviolent liberation: two men of different origin and with different starting points, but both striving toward the same goal.

My compatriot was much concerned with the awakening and fermenting continent which was to become his destiny. He once said that the next decade must belong to Africa or to the atom bomb. He firmly believed that the new countries have an important mission to fulfill in the community of nations. He therefore invested all his strength of will, and at the end more than that, to smooth their road toward the future.

Africa was to be the great test for the philosophy he wished to see brought to life through the United Nations.

Time and again he recurred to the indissoluble connection between peace and human rights. Tolerance, protection by law, equal political rights, and equal economic opportunities for all citizens - were prerequisites for a harmonious life within a nation. They also became requirements for such a life among nations.

He would remind us how man once organized himself in families, how families joined together in tribes and villages, and how tribes and villages developed into peoples and nations. But the nation could not be the end of such development. In the Charter of the United Nations he saw a guide to what he called an organized international community.

With an intensity that grew stronger each year, he stressed in his annual reports to the General Assembly that the United Nations had to be shaped into a dynamic instrument in the service of development. In his last report, in a tone of voice penetrating because of its very restraint, he confronted those member states which were clinging to "the time-honored philosophy of sovereign national states in armed competition, of which the most that may be expected is that they achieve a peaceful coexistence". This philosophy did not meet the needs of a world of ever increasing interdependence, where nations have at their disposal armaments of hitherto unknown destructive strength. The United Nations must open up ways to more developed forms of international cooperation.

He dated this report August 17 of this year. It now stands as a last testament.

He found the words of the Charter concerning equal rights for all nations, large and small, filled with life and significance. Above all, it was the small nations, and especially the developing countries, which needed the United Nations for their protection and their future. This was why he refused to step down and to throw the organization to the winds when one of the large nations demanded his resignation.

It was impossible to witness that scene at the stormy

session of last year's General Assembly without recalling some words that he once wrote about his own father. "A man of firm convictions does not ask, and does not receive, understanding from those with whom he comes into conflict", he wrote about Hjalmar Hammarskjöld. "A mature man is his own judge. In the end, his only firm support is being faithful to his own convictions." How aptly these words applied to himself when he rose unhesitatingly to defend the idea of a truly international body of civil servants or to uphold the principles of the Charter in the Congo operation!

If he felt any uneasiness, then it was because questions dealing with the peace and welfare of peoples were being treated in an overheated atmosphere. And an eyewitness, looking at him sitting there, deeply serious, with the fingers of his right hand against his cheek, as they always were when he was listening intently, might find himself asking this question: What does he represent, that slender man up there behind the green marble desk? A tradition of polished quiet diplomacy doomed to drown in the rising tide of new clamor? Or is he, with his visions of a world community, a herald of the future?

The latter is what we would like to believe. He himself had no doubt about the convincing force of his ideals. He expressed it thus in the last article that he wrote: "Setbacks in trying to realize the ideal do not prove that the ideal is at fault."

Such a conviction must be based on a determined

philosophy of life. No one who met him could help noticing that he had a room of quiet within himself. Probably no one was ever able really to reach into that room.

But perhaps we can think that he found something that was essential to himself in the last book that he was engaged in translating, the powerful work *Ich und Du* (I and Thou), in which the Jewish philosopher Martin Buber sets forth his belief that all real living is meeting. He himself believed that there were invisible bridges on which people could meet as human beings above the confines of ideologies, races, and nations.

And perhaps we may dare to see something significant in the obscurity and seeming futility of what happened on that African September night. Scattered about in the debris of the airplane were some books. Among them was *Ich und Du*, with some pages just translated into Swedish. Just before the plane took off on its nocturnal flight, he had left behind with a friend Thomas à Kempis' *Imitation of Christ*. Tucked in the pages was the oath of office of the Secretary-General:

"I, Dag Hammarskjöld, solemnly swear to exercise in all loyalty, discretion and conscience the functions entrusted to me as Secretary-General of the United Nations, to discharge these functions and regulate my conduct with the interest of the United Nations only in view..."

Had he stood here today, he would, I believe, have had

something to say about service as a self-evident duty.

My fellow countryman became a citizen of the world. He was regarded as such by the people from whom he came. But on that cool autumn day of falling leaves when he was brought back to the Uppsala of his youth, he was ours again, he was back home. Shyly he had guarded his inner world, but at that moment the distance disappeared and we felt that he came very close to us.

Therefore, I can speak on behalf of an entire people when I submit our respectful thanks for the honor that has been bestowed today upon our fellow citizen, the greatest honor a man can have. The Peace Prize awarded to Dag Hammarskjöld will constitute a fund which will bear his name and which will be used for a purpose that was close to his heart.

§ MONSIEUR H

By Anna Ankar Barron [*]

It is late morning in the OPI typing pool at UN Headquarters in the summer of 1956, and I am half asleep, head on arms folded across the typewriter waiting for Norman Ho, Chris Ryder, Roger Bayldon, Alan Chang or anyone else at the editors' desk to bring me another press release to cut on stencil. Does anyone remember "Sin in Sweden," a full-page article in *Time* magazine that year, which became a national sensation? A popular "bachelor girl," I had been at El Morocco on a blind date until three a.m. and had sand in my eyes.

Suddenly I hear a whisper in my ear: "You're wanted on

[*] Anna (Ankar) Barron's article first appeared in the Quarterly Bulletin of the Association of International Civil Servants (Vol. XXXVI, No. 4, October 2005). Courtesy of Anna Barron and the Association of International Civil Servants (New York).

the 38th floor right away. Aase says the S-G wants to dictate some Swedish letters." Wide awake now, with trembling knees and sledge-hammering heart, I dash to the elevator, panting "38th, please!" to the elevator girl (those were the days).

For this to be intelligible, let me explain that I was a 29-year-old Swedish steno-typist who had neither nourished any hopes of using her mother tongue at the UN, nor setting her foot on the 38th floor. But this was 1956, and Dag Hammarskjöld was Secretary-General.

The top floor of the United Nations Secretariat building was holy ground, strictly guarded, and you had to have a pretty good reason to step out onto the luxurious, beige wall-to-wall carpet (the high-rise's only full length carpeted office corridor - a sensation in itself) and face Ole, the seven-foot Norwegian guard (gemuetlich and much loved, by the way). After identifying me, Ole left his sketch pad and showed me the way to the office of Aase Alm, Trygve Lie's Norwegian secretary, who had stayed on after his departure to serve his successor, who ushered me into the inner sanctum.

While I'm at it, let me memorialize Ole, who was not only a stunning towering presence, but a talented cartoonist. When he learned that I was leaving Headquarters for good (this would be my first in a series of three departures from various departments) to be with my ailing father in Sweden, Ole did a hilarious drawing of me playing the violin seated on a chair while typing with my toes, which was circulated with much merriment for everyone to sign; it has followed me across the seas many times and now hangs framed in my Connecticut home where I can nostalgically revisit the personalities behind the signatures of Dag Hammarskjöld, Andrew Cordier, Leo Malania, Victor Mills, Ralph Bunche, Brian Urquhart *et al* who held positions on the 38th floor at the time, and some of whose secretary I later became. Urquhart, a flute player and a fellow member of the UN Music Club, performed for the staff in our chamber group at lunchtime. I recall Brian (Mr. Urquhart then, of course) as a sweet, unassuming man, quick to deprecate his instrumental skills in true British fashion.

Like many other Secretariat employees, I had fooled myself into believing I was leaving the UN permanently - that I could actually be happy somewhere else. Before I knew it, little peaceful Sweden had bored me to death and I found myself back a year later to the welcoming screams of former colleagues, though now "demoted" to the Office of Legal Affairs on the 34th floor. I was to leave the UN "permanently" again twice, popping up in a different department each time, happy as a lark to be "back home."

But I digress. Aase introduced me to Hammarskjöld, who in Swedish fashion shook my hand - he had these aristocratic hands with slender fingers - with the typical Swedish blend of polite aloofness behooving a man in high position. Being myself very shy (Swedish women were raised to be humble back then), I modestly looked down at my feet without a word (you don't speak unless spoken to) and sat down, head in the steno pad ready for battle.

Do you realize what it meant for this Swedish girl to not only shake hands with, but work for one of the world's most famous men, whom she revered, like everyone else in "The House" - Hammarskjöld's affectionate term for the high-rise - in his private office? What especially caught my attention upon entering the inner sanctum was this enormous, bare desk with not a single object on it except a blotter, an ink stand and a telephone. Monsieur H(ache), as the French called him and which I immediately adopted as very hip (the most fitting word, though, not yet coined), was without the aid of any papers. I was in a state of panic, breaking out in a cold sweat as he kept pacing the floor of the very large room with his back turned on his walk to the opposite end, which made it almost impossible to hear him, since he was soft-spoken in the first place. (Throughout my secretarial career, I've often wondered if "dictators" assume their stenographers to be psychic.) To ask him to repeat would have been a sacrilege as well as revealing me as a nincompoop of monumental proportions. Whenever the phone rang, he'd pick it up and carry on an animated conversation; after hanging up, he didn't ask "Where were we?" like other mortals, but instead picked up exactly where he had left off.

All of Hammarskjöld's Swedish correspondence was with members of the Swedish Academy of Letters, "The Eighteen," of which he himself was one. This meant that he was consulted about who should receive the Nobel Prize in literature. At the time of my assistance, the discussion involved a poet with the pen name of St. John Perse. I believe he became the winner that year.

When Monsieur H had finished dictating, I was directed to an antique Swedish Smith Corona in a nearby office where I spent agonizing tear-drenched hours trying to decipher and divine what the Great Man had said. It didn't help that in those days, letters were typed with multiple carbons and that errors had to be erased on each copy (apparently Andrew Cordier's rule, adorable man though he was), inevitably leaving smudge marks. As though that weren't enough, I had been warned that each letter for the S-G's signature was held up to the light to check for erasures and that if a single one showed through, the letter had to be retyped regardless of length. (What sadist had told Aase to thus instruct? Surely not kind Monsieur H.) This nightmare had its bright spot in retrospect in that it made a nearly flawless typist out of me.

As I returned to Sweden a few months later, I was only required to serve as the Secretariat's Swedish steno-typist for a limited time (I believe that Inga Britta, who later married Victor Mills, assumed my vacated seat) which, however, enabled me to transcribe an address that Hammarskjöld, himself a skilled botanist, delivered on renowned botanist Carl von Linne to the Swedish Academy of Letters. It was later printed as a leaflet, a copy of which he signed for me with a few kind words of thanks - one of my most cherished souvenirs, which I keep in my Swedish copy of *Vägmärken* (*Markings*).

I also got a glimpse of this remarkable man's simplicity and thoughtfulness. He would receive mail from little old ladies in the Swedish countryside wishing him God's blessing in his important work, and would dictate a personal note of thanks to them.

Another fascinating experience I had during this period thanks to my nationality and knowledge of European languages was a part-time assignment in Hammarskjöld's Upper East Side apartment. His American bodyguard, Bill Ranallo, a high-school graduate who was killed along with him at N'dola, and whom I recall vividly as a friendly man deeply devoted to his boss, for some cruel, obscure reason had been given the task of doing an inventory of Hammarskjöld's private multilingual library for insurance purposes. An unmitigated disaster, the job was given to me for "correction," but developed instead into a copy editor's dream involving a complete revision. The opportunity for this Swedish girl to handle, volume by volume, the collection of one of "The Eighteen" on foreign soil every afternoon for several weeks was not only indescribably uplifting, it was also delightfully time-consuming in that each volume had to be removed for notation of author, title, publisher and year of issue. What made the experience even more enjoyable was that a silver tray with coffee and home-baked Swedish butter cookies was brought to me every afternoon by Gustaf or Nelly, Hammarskjöld's Swedish housekeepers, an Evangelical couple who so worshipped their master that they wept and praised the Lord each time his name was uttered.

I remember my awe at seeing Sir Edmund Hilary's axe on the wall above the fireplace in the living room. Dag Hammarskjöld was not only a botanist but also an avid mountaineer who had written a book about trekking in Sarek, the Lapland wilderness of northern Sweden, which kindled his interest in botanics. I keep a copy in my Stockholm island cabin and pull it out during each visit, along with the Linne and *Markings*, for that nostalgic walk down memory lane.

One of the saddest, most solemn and moving experiences of my life was attending Dag Hammarskjöld's funeral in the Upsala Cathedral. I happened to be in Sweden on leave when he died, and Aase sent me an invitation. A special train had been reserved from Stockholm to Upsala to accommodate the many foreign visitors. There was not a dry eye to be seen during the service, at which the Archbishop of Sweden officiated, in the huge sanctuary, full to capacity. The atmosphere was such that I can still feel my chest heaving from convulsive sobbing. On my way to the cathedral, across the churchyard I noted the expressions of shocked grief in the pale faces of Sverker Aström, the Swedish Ambassador to the UN and a personal friend of Hammarskjöld's, and Lennart Finnmark, his Swedish assistant at Headquarters, who happened to be walking next to me on the way in.

§ DAG HAMMARSKJÖLD AND THE RELATION OF LAW TO POLITICS

By Oscar Schachter *

The sudden and tragic death of Dag Hammarskjöld on September 17, 1961, evoked throughout almost the entire world a sense of grief and loss that was without parallel in recent times. In the tributes paid him there was universal recognition of his extraordinary personal qualities: the depth and brilliance of his intellect, his strength of spirit, dedication, courage, and incredible stamina. He was that rare, indeed almost incomparable, combination of a man who could act with energy, boldness and consummate skill in meeting the harsh conflicts of our time, and at the same time could lead a life of inner contemplation and

---

* Oscar Schachter's eulogy for Dag Hammarskjöld, published in a 1962 issue of The American Journal of International Law. Reproduced with permission from © The American Society of International Law.

aesthetic experience. For those privileged to work closely with him, he had a contagious vitality and zest which, even in the most discouraging moments, inspired renewed effort. He brought to these personal qualities a tough minded awareness of political realities and a talent for creative political innovation. The result was an era of international action in which the United Nations moved from the plane of words to that of deeds in facing some of the most perilous crises of this generation. It may well be that, with the death of Mr. Hammarskjöld, this era has come to a close, but it is not likely that its example will be forgotten.

While Dag Hammarskjöld's accomplishments have been justifiably regarded as essentially political and diplomatic, their implications for the development of international law merit special consideration. He regarded himself as a man of law, in part because of his formal legal training, in part, it seemed, because of his intellectual delight in the subtleties of legal analysis. There was also perhaps an element of personal sentiment in his attitude, for he had a manifest pride in his family's legal background and especially in the contribution made by his father, Hjalmar Hammarskjöld, and his brother Åke. Much more important, however, than these considerations was the conviction, which he increasingly expressed, that the processes of la, and, as he put it, the principles of justice were crucial to the effort to avert disaster and to achieve a secure and decent international order. That this conviction went far deeper than the conventional homage paid to the rule of law soon became evident to one who shared his professional interest. It was more than a belief in a distant goal; it inspired and influenced his actions from day to day, and it is not surprising that one of the first tributes paid him by an ambassador who knew him well was to describe him as "imbued with the spirit of law."

It may be asked whether the "spirit of law" or a belief in the value of the legal process can have much practical significance in an intensely political atmosphere such as that of the United Nations. There are, of course, many who answer in the negative; they see no meaningful application of law except in terms of an effective judicial system, and they regard references to "law" in a political body as no more than rhetorical flourishes without influence on actual conduct or policy. Hammarskjöld's beliefs and his practical actions were in a sense a challenge to this view, for they affirmed the importance of law in the United Nations while acknowledging the realities of power and political pressures. To demonstrate this more specifically, an attempt will be made to summarize, under four headings, what seem to be the fundamental conceptions of Hammarskjöld's approach to the relation of law and politics in contemporary international society. These conceptions, it will be seen, differ substantially from the traditional views of international lawyers and place in fresh perspective some of the pervasive dilemmas of international politics.

1. Law as a Source and Basis of Policy

Hammarskjöld made no sharp distinction between law

and politics; in this he departed clearly from the prevailing positivist approach. He viewed the body of law not merely as a technical set of rules and procedures, but as the authoritative expression of principles that determine the goals and direction of collective action. This did not mean, of course, that he considered that legal precepts alone express the aims of states, or that they automatically determine the decisions of international bodies irrespective of other considerations. He recognized that, in international society as in domestic, legal norms are one class of many factors that enter into the process of decision-making. But, while acknowledging the influence of other factors, he laid stress on the binding character of the legal element, and consequently on the priority that should be accorded to it over other interests and claims. This was not merely a theoretical point of view: his record is replete with instances in which he found that the principles of the Charter, general and comprehensive as they are, provided sufficient guidance to enable him to resolve concrete controversies. Faced with conflicting national demands and expectations, he relied on these principles and on other generally accepted legal concepts as a manifestation of the long-range major policies to which all governments had committed themselves. He did this not merely in deference to formal authority, but on the premise that the fundamental principles of the Charter and international law embodied the deeply-held values of the great majority of mankind and therefore constituted the moral, as well as the legal, imperatives of international life. In the main, he saw them "as a projection into the international arena and international community of purposes and principles already accepted as being of national validity."

2. Principles and Flexibility

Hammarskjöld's reliance on principles and legal concepts may appear to be at variance with the flexibility and adroitness that characterized much of his political activity; yet on reflection it will be seen that these apparently antithetical approaches were both essential aspects of a skilled technique for dealing with the specific problems which he faced. It is a technique that should be of special interest to the international lawyer, for it demonstrated that legal norms can be applied to novel situations without rigidity or blind conformity to precedent.

That Hammarskjöld was able to do this maybe attributed to three factors. One was that his own cast of mind and philosophic approach were congenial to the interplay between principles and contingent fact; he variably sought for norms but he was equally mindful of the variety, flux and novelty of actual events. A second factor was his conception of his office. A fundamental tenet was that the exclusively international responsibility of the Secretary-General implied above all a firm adherence to the principles of the Charter and other standards accepted as binding by Member States. Only through principled behavior could he fulfill his obligation of impartiality and avoid the risks of partisan and special pleading.

At the same time he realized that he was not a judge, called upon to pass judgment on the propriety of state conduct. He regarded himself essentially as a diplomat, a political technician who was required from time to time to deal with specific problems. The fact that these problems arose frequently in situations of crisis was the third factor influential in Hammarskjöld's approach. For the element of "crisis" meant that there was strong pressure to meet the necessities of the particular problem and to avoid the adoption of formulae that might have unforeseen implications in future cases. It was this third factor that called for the "ad hoc" solution and the supple application of general rules.

The technique of fusing these opposing elements into workable solutions cannot be easily described; it is more art than engineering and blueprints are not likely to be available. Certainly, an essential feature lay in the nature of the general rules which guided him. They were, in the main, principles derived from Articles 1 and 2 of the Charter; on that basis, they already commanded, in a psychological and political sense, high priority among the values formally accepted by the governments of the world. They were flexible in that they did not impose specific patterns or detailed machinery for action; they left room for adaptation to the particular needs and the resources available for a given undertaking.

A good example is seen in the guiding principles which Hammarskjöld derived from the experience of the United Nations Emergency Force in Gaza, and which he summarized in a report to the General Assembly. He cautioned against a mechanical repetition of the UNEF formula, and indicated the factors which might require a different pattern in the future. However, he also considered that, by distilling the UNEF experience, it was possible to arrive at fundamental criteria which would provide standards and guidelines for future undertakings and consequently facilitate their adoption by the United Nations organs. It was not long before this was tested in the Security Council proceedings dealing with the request for military assistance in the Congo. The precise UNEF arrangement did not fit the Congo, but the guiding principles derived from that experience were advanced by the Secretary-General and accepted by the governments as the constitutional basis of the United Nations operation in the Congo. The principles included that of non-intervention in internal political conflicts, the exclusion of the major military Powers from the Force, the international character and status of the Force, the independence of the United Nations in the selection of such troops, and the concept of good faith in the interpretation of the purposes of the Force. The fact that these principles had been formulated in advance enabled the Secretary-General at the outset to clarify the legal and practical basis of the Force for the Congo and provided a strengthened foundation for action by the governments. General as these principles might appear to be when stated in the abstract, the experience in the Congo demonstrated that they could have effect in projecting specific policies to be followed and in restraining ill-conceived measures.

It is also of significance in evaluating Hammarskjöld's flexibility that he characteristically expressed basic principles in terms of opposing tendencies (applying, one might say, the philosophic concept of polarity or dialectical opposition). He never lost sight of the fact that a principle, such as that of observance of human rights, was balanced by the concept of non-intervention, or that the notion of equality of states had to be considered in a context which included the special responsibilities of the great Powers. The fact that such precepts had contradictory implications meant that they could not provide automatic answers to particular problems, but rather that they served as criteria which had to be weighed and balanced in order to achieve a rational solution of the particular problem. Paul Freund gave eloquent expression to this idea in regard to the abstractions in American constitutional law:

"These abstractions, arrayed in intransigent hostility like robot sentinels facing each other across a border, can become useful guardians on either hand in the climb to truth if they can be made to march together. Somehow the life blood of the concrete problem tempers the mechanical arrogance of abstractions."

While this theme was not explicitly formulated by Hammarskjöld, it runs through his statements and his actions. He recognized that there was inevitably a tension between principles and concrete needs; his actions showed that, by taking account of both, he sought to achieve "that combination of steadfastness of purpose and flexibility of approach which alone can guarantee that the possibilities which we are exploring will have been tested to the full."

3. The Relation between Law and Diplomacy

Hammarskjöld conceived of his office primarily in terms of diplomacy, a "quiet" diplomacy which he conducted, as Walter Lippmann observed, with "a finesse and courtliness in the great tradition of Europe." Bu the setting and purposes of that diplomacy were far from the traditional. In Lippmann's eloquent appraisal: "Never before and perhaps never again has any man used the intense art of diplomacy for such unconventional and novel experiments." Whether unconventional or traditional, diplomacy is normally regarded as separate from – indeed, some would say opposed to – the processes of law, and many have warned against mingling the two. Yet the experience of Hammarskjöld indicates that this is an oversimplified view, and that a properly balanced combination of law and diplomacy may be and advantage, even at times a necessity.

The advantage of a legal basis is perhaps most evident when one considers the initial stage of a conciliation or good offices effort. It is apparent that a third party cannot enter the delicate terrain of inter-state controversy without having a *locus standi* acceptable to the parties directly concerned. Sometimes this is simply satisfied by the willingness of the parties to accept a friendly third-party intermediary; far more frequently, there are objections to any conciliation efforts, and influential groups within the states concerned (or perhaps external forces) may take it difficult for the governments to agree to a third-party "volunteer." However, when the third party is buttressed by firm legal authority – that is, when his *locus standi* rests on the rules and procedures to which that state has formally committed itself, that in itself becomes a cogent factor in overcoming resistance. Diplomatic intervention may then be viewed as part of generally accepted procedures agreed to by all states, and consequently involving no invidious connotation for the party to the dispute. Hammarskjöld had a profound appreciation of this aspect of peaceful settlement, and he therefore attached considerable importance to the grant of authority enabling him to enter into private discussions. He recognized in this respect the legal significance of the Security Council's responsibilities under the Charter, and he laid stress on the importance of a mandate by that organ in situations involving threats to the peace. In point of fact, most of his diplomatic activities, notably in the Middle East, Africa and Southeast Asia, were undertaken on the basis of a mandate of the Security Council, bolstered in several cases by agreements of the parties themselves. Only rarely did he offered his good offices without a Security Council or General Assembly mandate, and these instances were limited to situations in which both sides desired his participation in preliminary discussions.

There is another, no less important, aspect of the relation between law and diplomacy which can be discerned in

Hammarskjöld's diplomatic technique. An examination of his conciliation efforts shows that he relied to a considerable extent on establishing a common ground of principles to which both sides could adhere. An essential element in this process was to suggest general standards which had a legal quality, whether as an accepted norm of international law or as a rule which was implied by or closely related to a principle of law. The legal aspect was important in achieving acceptance because it endowed the proposed standards with the authority of pre-existing obligations and the character of a universal rule that would be applied equally in other cases. It thus implied that the solution to be reached would not diverge too sharply from the probable expectations of the states concerned, and for that reason was less likely to involved political difficulties. It also offered an assurance that the conciliation effort was carried out with objectivity and impartiality and therefore without discrimination against either side. Hammarskjöld's awareness of these factors is demonstrated by his frequent recourse to legal rules and precedents which, directly or by analogy, could be applied to the particular situation and accepted as guiding principles by the parties concerned. By a discriminating and skillful use of legal principles, he was thus able to further his diplomacy of conciliation and by its success to reinforce the effectiveness of law.

4. Law, Power and Action

Although Hammarskjöld often stressed the imperative quality of legal norms, this did not mean that he regarded law as an autonomous force which develops and is applied independently of political and social factors. He preferred to view law not as a "construction of ideal patterns," but in an "organic sense," as an institution which grows in response to felt necessities and within the limits set by historical conditions and human attitudes. Placed as he was in the center of the political maelstrom, Hammarskjöld could not but be keenly aware of the impact of power relations on the normative structure of international society. He was especially mindful of the fact that the constitutional pattern of the United Nations had been molded largely by the concentration of power in the two major blocs and by the deep conflict between them. He was equally aware of the extent to which internal instability and the demands for radical changes affected the application of existing rules of public order. But it was characteristic that he regarded these factors not merely as imposing limits on the use of law, but in a more positive sense as a challenge which called for creative attempts to find new norms and procedures. In making these attempts in new directions, Hammarskjöld never lost sight of the limiting conditions; he always was conscious that he was nurturing an organic growth, not designing an ideal pattern.

He did not, therefore, attempt to set law against power. He sought rather to find within the limits of power the elements of common interest on the basis of which joint action and agreed standards could be established. In the area of advancing technologies, such as atomic energy and outer space, he pursuit efforts to develop new normative arrangements based on the acknowledged factors of interdependence. In the economic and social field, he stressed the mutual interest of the advanced states in combating the debasement of living standards and the human dignity in the impoverished countries of the world. In the most critical arena, the relation between the major power blocs, he devoted himself to seeking balanced arrangements based on the mutual interest of both blocs to survive in a world in which each posses the power to destroy the other. He did not endeavor to enter directly into big Power-relations, nor in any way to mediate directly between them. But he found opportunities in the peripheral areas, especially in the "power vacuums" that arose in underdeveloped areas and which provoked external intervention and the inevitable counteraction by the other side. In these matters he sought to stave off the dangerous spiral of action and reaction by measures to fill the vacuums and create a viable economy and government by means of economic and financial aid, the building of governmental and administrative machinery, the provision of educational and technical training, and, even as in the Congo, by using armed force to maintain internal order. These measures, commonly described as "executive actions," signified for Hammarskjöld a fundamental decisive advance toward a more effective system of international cooperation, and they have been widely regarded as constituting a major feature of his political legacy.

Although these "operational" measures do not at first

seem to be related to international law, it will be evident on reflection that they have an impact on the evolution of standards of international behavior, and the effective implementation of such standards. For it must be borne in mind the collective intervention of the kind described, based on United Nations principles, involve more than "action." It necessarily includes new conceptions of permissible and impermissible interference by individual states, and of the Charter obligations for mutual assistance and cooperation. Moreover, such measures constitute, as Mr. Hammarskjöld observed, practical means and techniques for bringing about compliance with international decisions and principles. They can, therefore, be regarded in a broader and more subtle sense, as a part of the enforcement or sanctioning machinery which is available to the international community to assure observance of its decisions. Viewed in these terms, such practical action will be seen as imparting a new dimension to the efforts to give vigor and efficacy to a normative structure based on the common interests of all peoples.

ANGELA E.V. KING

Matthew Couper
Angela King
2011
Pencil on paper
7" x 5" / 175mm x 135mm
www.mattcouper.com

Angela E. V. King *2003

1938 ~ 2007

* from a photograph by
Olga Bobrova (aka Oleykha)

38 years in the United Nations.

Matthew Cooper 2022

"A fervent champion of the equality of women and men, and women's enjoyment of their human rights, she knew that all parts of the United Nations had a responsibility to uphold those principles, -- including in the area of peace and security. Ms. King's advocacy and partnership with civil society paved the way for the Security Council's landmark resolution 1325 (2000) on women, peace and security -- the Council's first recognition of women's essential role in peacebuilding, peacemaking and peace negotiations."

— *Ban Ki-moon*
Secretary-General
of the United Nations

§ A WOMAN OF THE UNITED NATIONS

By Andreas Sandre von Warburg and Erika Suban [*]

– On March 8, 2006, then Secretary-General Kofi Annan said: "The world is ready for a woman Secretary-General." For the first time, the Organization was opening the doors of the highest-level position to women. What was your first reaction?

– I was actually very pleased. It was the first time a Secretary-General – to my knowledge – has ever said on International Women's Day – or any other day for that matter – that the United Nations is ready for a woman Secretary-General. But then I stopped and thought about it: if this was really to have had an impact, he should have started saying it at least three to five years ago, when he got re-elected. Well, I suppose better late than ever!

---

[*] Excerpt from an interview given by Angela King in the summer of 2006.

– Assuming that the world is ready for a woman Secretary-General, do you think the United Nations is ready?

– I think the United Nations will never be ready for a woman Secretary-General until it has a woman at the top. It has to have a woman Secretary-General first. The UN is quite an archaic organization, and very hierarchical. And it has been over the years and still is very male-chauvinistic and male-oriented. I still have a deep feeling that only men can be successful.

– The United Nations has many qualified women for the top level position of the UN. Do you think a woman – and I mean a staff member, just like Kofi Annan was – would ever been considered for the Secretary-General post?

– The way the United Nations works, very few Secretaries-General have come from within the Secretariat. In fact, Kofi Annan was really the only one. Javier Perez de Cuellar worked in the Secretariat for a really short period, but I'm not sure you can really count that. The candidates really come from countries and ultimately from regions – and according to customary rules, the next Secretary-General should be from Asia.

It is a question for the delegations to consider putting forward a woman. However, one should plan for the long term – you cannot start a campaign six or 12 months before the election. I am very proud of Equality Now. They have took up the cudgels and put forward a list of women from Asia and other countries who could certainly do the task.

Again, as I said earlier, it is not a question of when the United Nations will be ready for a woman at the top. It has to be imposed by Member States, by the voting Membership. If we wait for the UN to be ready, we will never have a woman Secretary-General.

– Why are there so little women at the Under-Secretary-General and Assistant Secretary-General levels?

– My feeling is that the United Nations has big doubts about women. You always hear that they cannot find women or when they find women who are qualified for top-level positions they turn them down or their husband is working somewhere else, or so on. However, if you take on average the women who are asked vis-à-vis the men who are asked, the ones who turn an offer down are very few. In other words, I feel there has been a total lack of a proper search machine for high-level women. There has also been a total lack of seeking out and following up. In other words, since the UN revolves around a men-centered boy's network, people know a lot of men in international affairs, they don't know women. There are mechanisms that have been suggested that key women be brought up to the United Nations either in Geneva, Addis Ababa, or New York and interviewed so that when post becomes available there is a core of 15-20 women who are able to fill vacancies in peacekeeping, development or any variety of posts. But it is still limping along as in "I know this person" or "this government puts forward that person" or you have to have that nationality so it's not been systematic at all.

– The last report of the Secretary-General to the General Assembly (A/59/357) on the "Improvement of the status of women in the United Nations System" points out that the Secretariat "continues to view these policies (work/life policies to attract and retain quality staff) as a barrier to efficiency and productivity and, more importantly, as incompatible with career advancement and the performance of managerial level posts." Do you think women are discriminated against at the United Nations?

– I think women are discriminated against at the United Nations, indeed. If you look at large corporation in this country, in the United States, in the developed countries and even in many developing countries, such as Brazil, accommodations are being made for women with children or elderly parents or other special situations; there is a much greater flexibility with women working from home or time off policies – look at the Scandinavian countries. The UN has not quite reached that point. On paper there are several provisions that would lead you to think that women for example can work at home just as men can, or that they can take time-off or maternity leave; but in reality, if they do, it is often believed and it seems to be held against them in terms of career advancement.

– *"Gender imbalance is a multidimensional and systemic problem which requires a systemic and integrated response,"* as the Secretary-General points out in the report. What would this systemic and integrated response be? And how the United Nations is trying to respond to gender issues, especially for high-level positions?

– Generally speaking, the United Nations has some procedures that are supposed to take care of gender equality imbalances and equal opportunities for women and men. In fact, they have been in place for a good two decades at least. In particular, these have partly been put in place by enlightened Member States.

It is imperative that the Organization commit itself to create equal opportunities for qualified women in the Secretariat – I'm not talking exclusively about New York, but in all duty stations, such as Geneva, Addis Ababa, Bangkok, Rome and so on – in terms of promotion, career development, and consideration for new assignments – it is not just a question of promotion. And the UN has to ensure that women who meet the qualifications for high-level posts are appointed.

However, under the "Convention for the Elimination of any form of Discrimination against Women" – which is a women's rights convention – there is a provision in article 4 that special measures to promote women and to improve the situation of women within the Secretariat are in order until parity is reached. Let me repeat: until parity is reached. The Secretaries-General in the past have used this provision to institute special measures; for example: women who applied would be given preference; regular recruitment missions were formed in order to try to bring on board women – I've been to such missions in China and Russia, where traditionally they put forward only male candidates for vacant posts. This was in the Nineties and things have changed a little now.

In the last five or so years, these special measures have been ignored. There was a sort of blasé attitude of satisfaction. In other words, having reached higher percentage numbers of women, managers didn't bother to look for more women – "why bother, women are everywhere" sort of attitude. And unfortunately, this took place while the Office for Human Resources was headed by a woman, and the office of Administration and Management was headed by a woman. In my office, as the Special Adviser to the Secretary-General, we tried our best to ensure that some modicum of special measures were still in place. Some remained in place, but quite honestly the United Nations has not followed this up.

§ MUCH REMAINS TO BE DONE

By Angela E.V. King [*]

This is the last time that I shall be writing to you as Special Adviser for Gender Issues and Advancement of Women. After nearly 38 years in the Organization, I am leaving for a new life and new challenges. I have seen many changes—changes for the better—both qualitative and quantitative in terms of the de facto equality of women and men in the UN.

When I arrived here the day after Labour Day in 1966, there were few women at the Professional level: few D-1s, even fewer D-2s, and none at the Assistant Secretary-General or Under-Secretary-General levels. The first

[*] Angela E.V. King's farewell letter as Special Adviser of the Secretary-General on Gender Issues and Advancement of Women (published in Network - The UN Women's Newsletter, Vol. 8, No. 1, January, February and March 2004)

woman to break the ceiling as ASG was Ms. Helvi Sipila, Finland's first woman lawyer and a redoubtable professional in her own right, with a background in public service, human rights and women's advancement. She was appointed ASG for Social Development and Humanitarian Affairs in 1972.

From the UN's inception, but more particularly since the 1970s, the General Assembly, the Commission on the Status of Women, the four World Conferences on Women and the Special Session, Beijing+5, and other UN bodies have routinely recognized the innate unfairness of condoning unequal opportunities for women inside an Organization professing fundamental human rights and equal opportunities for all people—women, men, youth and children—throughout the world.

We have come a long way towards the goal of reaching 50/50 women and men set first by Secretary-General Boutros Boutros-Ghali and then by the Beijing Conference and the General Assembly in 1995 during the Fiftieth Anniversary of the United Nations. Today, we have reached 37 per cent on overall posts with staff having contracts of one year or more, and 42.5 per cent on posts subject to geographical distribution. Progress was made in women's appointments to high-level and decision-making positions. The second highest position in the Organization, that of Deputy Secretary-General, is held by a woman. There are women heading Secretariat entities, such as UN-Habitat, ECE, ESCWA, the Department of Management and the Office of the High Commissioner for Human Rights.

In the UN system, over the last 10 or so years, women have headed WHO, UNHCR and WFP, and still head UNICEF and UNFPA. A woman is Prosecutor of the International Tribunal for the Former Yugoslavia and another woman is Vice-President of the International Criminal Court . These gains are in no small measure owing to the leadership of the Secretary- General, of many progressive programme managers, male and female, of the persistent advocacy by the Group of Equal Rights for Women in the UN, of changing attitudes, and of mechanisms such as my Office, including the Focal Point for Women, the departmental focal points, the special measures for the achievement of gender equality and accountability mechanisms, such as the gender and human resources action plans.

Another mechanism which is often forgotten is the Group of Women Ambassadors, now numbering nine, but which numbered zero four decades ago. This Group, initially formed by Ms. Madeleine Albright, has spearheaded a number of initiatives, including encouraging gender sensitivity in peace missions and repeatedly proposing more women appointees as Special Representatives of the Secretary-General in peace operations.

Despite this notable progress over nearly 40 years, much remains to be done. Gender stereotyping is still commonplace, with women staff not always considered on an equal footing to men for promotions, appointments, plum assignments, missions and special post allowances, for example. Flexi-time, which has been proven to enhance job satisfaction and productivity, is granted grudgingly and often with the lingering threat of less than fair appraisals. Harassment and abuse of power, including sexual harassment, are still not taken as seriously as we wish they should be. Although harassment is declared unacceptable, women's complaints are often still ignored or dismissed. The General Service staff, comprising over 60 per cent women, is virtually locked out of a progressive career path. Finally, we need to create a "critical mass" of women in policy-and decision-making and, thus, many more women need to be appointed to senior-level positions. To overcome these obstacles, we need to implement a well-known set of formulae: strong commitment and leadership by example in promoting gender equality; real accountability with sanctions and praise; solidarity on the part of women in partnership with like-minded men; workable mentoring schemes at all levels and at all duty stations; compulsory gender-sensitivity training; advocacy and vigilance; and a great deal of coordination and teamwork. We are happy to learn that Ms. Elisabeth Lindenmayer, the newly appointed and first woman Deputy Chef de Cabinet, is responsible for women's issues. Responsible units have to work together. These include the Office of the Secretary-General, OUSG/ DM, DM/OHRM, OSAGI/Focal Point for Women and all Chiefs of Administration and Personnel.

At this point, in addition to Ms. Helvi Sipila, I would like to mention a few of the women who may have been forgotten, but who have stood out in the past in the long fight for women's rights in the Secretariat: Ms. Pat Tsien and Ms. Claire de Hedervary, the first two Presidents of what is now the Group of Equal Rights for Women; Ms. Mercedes de Briceno, the first Coordinator for the Improvement of the Status of Women in the Secretariat; and Focal Points, Ms. Susan Habachy, Ms. Parin Mohamedi and Ms. Zohreh (ZuZu) Tabatabai. As we forge ahead into this new century, gains have to be consolidated and progress continued. There is no place for complacency, as grounds gained in gender equality can be swiftly and insidiously lost. As I start a new phase of my life, with some trepidation, I might add, I take heart in the warmth and fellowship that working at the UN and with you have brought me personally. I wish you, all of you, the best in your careers and the courage to keep fighting for your convictions and for the ideals and principles on which the United Nations is based.

§ WOMEN, PEACE, AND POSTS – IN UNITED NATIONS PEACE
OPERATIONS

By Angela E.V. King[†]

It is a pleasure to see that the momentum of Security
Council resolution 1325 (2000) generated six years ago still
continues with no loss of commitment, energy or drive on
the part of the international community. For this I
commend those Council members who have consistently
raised the issue of women's contributions to peace and
security. I would also like to thank those Council Presidents
who propelled the issue forward, the Department of
Peacekeeping Operations (DPKO), the Office of the
Special Adviser (OSAGI), key UN agencies and bodies in

[†] Angela King's address to the United Nations panel discussion co-hosted by the
Office of the Special Advisor of the Secretary-General on Gender Issues and the
U.N. Department of Peacekeeping Operations (October 25, 2006) on the occasion of
the 6th anniversary of U.N. Security Council Resolution 1325 (S/RES/1935 –
October 31, 2000) on women, peace, and security.

the field, the non-governmental organizations and not least----the Inter-Agency Task Force on Women, Peace and Security.

My input to the debate on Women, Peace and Posts, will be in two parts. The first is challenges I faced as a woman Chief of the United Nations Observer Mission in South Africa (UNOMSA), 1992-1994, and second, strategies I devised for achieving a high ratio of women on posts resulting in the final stages of the mission with women serving on 50% of the regional director posts. Here, I add some practical proposals for improving the current disappointingly low figure of 30% women in peace operations and especially those at higher levels.

It may be useful to recall that the apartheid system in South Africa had started to crumble with the release of Nelson Mandela from prison in 1990 and the subsequent talks between leaders of the ruling National Party and those of the African National Congress (ANC), the Pan-Africanist Congress (PAC) and others about the future path of the country. This was a time of frequent murders, high incidence of rape, violence, both white-on-black and vice versa and black-on-black, train and taxi riots and bombings, public beatings, police brutality and arbitrary incarceration. At the same time, political refugees were returning to swell the ranks of the disaffected and unemployed. Above all there was crushing poverty among the vast majority of the population. Non-whites felt deeply bitter at years of injustice. Whites felt deep anxiety about violence, loss of statusand expropriations of property similar to what took place in Rhodesia and Kenya. Combined, these resentments created an atmosphere of palpable and dangerous tension.

The Boipatong massacre in May 1992 led to the breakdown of the Convention for a Democratic South Africa (CODESA). Followed closely by the Bisho massacre in September, the Security Council was finally obliged to take tangible action. The Council by resolution 772 decided to send a small mission to observe at first hand what was happening on the ground and to report back regularly. As South Africa was then under economic sanctions to end apartheid, there was no formal UN presence in the country except the office of the United Nations High Commissioner for Refugees (UNHCR) assisting with placing returning refugees.

The leaders of the ruling National Party and other conservative elements strongly opposed our mission. They considered that South Africans could resolve their own problems without external interference. Members of the ANC and others, on the other hand, who had regularly testified on the state of affairs before the Special Committee on Against Apartheid, wanted a mission comprised of at least 5,000 military and police. So they too felt deeply disappointed and resentful of the UN.

This was the somewhat tense and hostile atmosphere into which the first 13 members of UNOMSA, arrived in September 1992..

As a woman Chief of Mission I experienced three main challenges. The first was to convince national leaders (political, religious, unionists), that the UN had come to work with them on the road to sustainable peace and racial equality rather than to dictate terms. To do this I set myself the task of meeting with all 28 political entities. I met 24 including the leaders of the main parties, President de Klerk, Nelson Mandela, Chief Mangosutho Buthelezi, Clarence Makwetu, HM King Zwethilini of the Zulus and the heads of all ten Bantustans. I sought advice from various religious leaders such as Archbishop Desmond Tutu and leading academicians and writers.

We were assisted in settling in and determining targets by the peace structures set up under the Peace Accord signed by 27 of thel parties in September 1991. Many of these structures to promote peace at national, regional and local levels, however, did not yet exist and where they did, they represented the ruling ethnic profile rather than the wealth of ethnic and political diversity, gender balance and youth. One of our tasks became strengthening and democratizing these entities.

As Chief of Mission, I was seen as a UN official, black, and from a very small island, Jamaica. (Apart from reggae, rum and the cricket), I thus had several counts against me. The most significant challenge, however, was being a woman. It was seen as a bit of a let-down, but in the Secretary-General's eyes perfectly in harmony with a "very low-key" mission. In South Africa, women, while at the forefront of the fight against apartheid, were still not generally aroused to fight for their own equal rights with men--- in parliament, the home and the workplace. As each of the entities gradually realized that we treated them equally: attending events where our presence was likely to diffuse violence such as functions and funerals, marches, fearlessly challenging the police on the use of dogs and guns against marchers, and so on, our impartiality was accepted. Confidence in us grew, doors opened everywhere and the invitations from our warm-hearted, and curious hosts, became almost too numerous.

I soon found that with the substantial number of women observers and myself, as a woman Chief, we had a strong unforeseen affinity with the women of the community. They were impressed by the fact that more than men, we listened seriously to their needs, their views of the situation and their possible solutions. As a result they were more open than the men to accept and pass on to their communities and families, our suggestions for achieving peace. South African women became our strongest allies and collaborators for peace. Women often gave UNOMSA women early warnings of areas where violence was likely to break out. We could then either offset the threats or diffuse them, working with the other missions, the police or our Peace Accord partners.

I must emphasize that involving local women as equals in achieving peace was one of our most successful policies and should be an integral built-in mandate and concept of every mission. A spin-off, according to one of our regional directors, could be that in similar missions, local women treated equally, could gain a higher status vis a vis the mission and males particularly the military and police, might then regard them with greater respect than has been the case of several recent missions.

Another point of contention in been accepted was the term "observer". The local population felt that we were there "to watch them being killed" rather than to stop the killings. We were held in great contempt until we proved that "observing" could morph effectively into low-key "facilitating", "negotiating" and proposing viable options to achieve peace. We "lucked out", however, with our acronym, UNOMSA, which means "She who brings mercy" in Zulu, the language spoken by the majority of South Africans.

As Chief of Mission the main aspect of this challenge was convincing people of our willingness to help and assuring them that the UN wanted them to succeed. We had to be scrupulously fair and impartial, whether in praising restraint or in condemning violence. Once this was established, I had no problems in gaining access to any of the leaders. Some of course were more gracious than others and I well remember when we visited Ciskei at the Cabinet's invitation, we were held for an hour at gunpoint before being permitted to enter.   I also recall our team being imprisoned in Bophuthatswana on Ascension Day 1993. We were finally vouched for by the head of the National Peace Committee and allowed to depart.

The second challenge as a woman Chief of Mission was

dealing with Headquarters' hierarchy. Then as now, there lingers in the minds of many male staff as part of the UN culture, the patronizing conviction, subconscious or otherwise, that women are not equal to men especially when it comes to sharing crucial political information. "Need to know" almost always excludes women.

While irritating, women, forced to develop a counter-competency, always have a way of finding out what is really important.

I was asked to head the South African mission at 7.30 p.m. one night. I had 24 hours to decide. Having been a leader of a march of students from the University of the West Indies in downtown Kingston to protest the Sharpeville massacre in 1960, and as a Jamaican whose country had initiated the proposal at a Commonwealth Heads of Government meeting to adopt sanctions against South Africa, I had only one answer. Yes. This mission proved to be the most challenging and fulfilling experience of my nearly 38-year career at the UN.

The team's briefing at Headquarters, prior to departure, was sketchy. Luckily on arrival, the National Peace Committee briefed us thoroughly on all aspects of our mandate and on the situation and the culture. We replicated this information to other observers as they arrived and had daily meetings to hear news from other duty stations. The UNOMSA team gradually grew to 500 in 60 locations and finally to just over 2,000 prior to the April 1994 first, non-racial, democratic elections.

There was very little by way of day to day or even weekly instructions from New York, and with a small team of advisers and biweekly reports from all the teams scattered at flashpoints throughout the country, with our team leaders, we learned to work together by intuition, knowledge and the seat of our pants.

As part of Headquarters strategy at the time to counter widely held criticisms that the UN's policy for achieving peace in Africa was just not working, the then Secretary-General brought his three heads of mission in Africa: Angola, Mozambique and South Africa together to a meeting in Maputo.   I was included as an equal in all the closed meetings at which he firmly told the recalcitrant opposition leaders in Mozambique that they had to be reasonable or he would withdraw all United Nations forces and assistance. Ironically, I was nevertheless excluded from the Presidential Palace for a State Dinner for us that evening, as security decided that "women did not belong there". (I eventually made it before the dessert.)

In my opinion, whenever male chauvinism embedded in the Secretariat and in peace operations is totally eliminated--- and it must be---, women Chiefs or SRSGs already performing at top levels, will be able to devote even more quality time to their official jobs then to fending off petty slights and humiliations.

For me the third challenge as a woman Chief was how to

mould into a coherent team, individuals from different departments and disciplines, different parts of the UN system, with those from outside of the UN ranging from former foreign ministers to students, innocent of the UN culture. I approached this challenge through orientation, personal knowledge of each staff, strict respect for local norms and customs and to their personal security. In order to deploy teams to major areas of conflict, we had teams of two or three, usually with a balance of gender, disciplines, and ethnicity. To offset the vast distances between headquarters and most of the teams and to heighten morale, the regional directors and I were in contact with each team leader as frequently as possible.

We tried as far as possible to recruit versatile staff with prior mission experience and knowledge of the political situation. Given the context of South Africa then, the mixed teams were particularly useful in demonstrating that a mix of race and gender could work harmoniously---an essential ingredient for achieving and maintaining peace. This factor was ingrained in me coming from a highly multiracial society, Jamaica, where racial prejudices existed, but which I had observed lessened, incrementally.

For the first time a Chief of a UN mission had to coordinate all three teams from the European Union (all male military or police), the African Union (all male) and the Commonwealth (mixed). Most of our pre-planning work for operations in the field was done jointly. The UN appreciated the additional military and police expertise in these teams which greatly enhanced our overall capacity and strategic approach.

We communicated with Headquarters mainly by regular bi-monthly reports for the Secretary-General and the Council. These were based on an overall analysis of what was occurring in all 60 duty stations drawn from their reports and on trends in the country as a whole.

There was a very human side to the mission as important perhaps as the political. As a non-family mission, there were men who pined for their wives, women who missed their husbands and children, staff with financial problems or those worried about the fidelity of significant others left at home. Others failed to take medications or turned to alcohol when under stress. We dealt with these on an individual basis and as quickly as possible as a single case could affect the morale of the entire mission. Luckily, I had the services of a very competent OHRM personnel officer at the beginning of the mission who helped me to recognize when an observer was over-stressed, disruptive or taking too many risks. We devised special Rest and Recreation packages for these instances. In some cases a recall to the parent duty station was the only solution.

Overall, joint participation and distribution of information on what strategies or innovative ideas succeeded or failed among other teams, drew the teams together and facilitated a common approach to our work. May I say that I had a truly outstanding group of people working with me whether as observers, electoral officers, spokespersons, radio operators, transport specialists or administrators. Whilst a dozen years have passed, members of the UNOMSA team still meet on the anniversary of the first elections for a celebratory dinner in New York. I may also say that this mission was judged in a 1993/4 mission of the International Peace Academy the first successful mission of preventive diplomacy in the context of Boutros Ghali's 1992 *Agenda for Peace.*

The second part of my statement deals with strategies used for getting more women into UNOMSA where we had over 46% during the first 18 months and where 50% were Regional Directors in the final and most dangerous phase just prior to the elections. I cannot stress how important was the close collaboration I had with OHRM. As a former Director of Recruitment and of Staff Administration and Training I encountered many staff. I found that I knew people from all over the Secretariat including other duty stations. This knowledge was enhanced by my 3-4 yearly lateral moves within several areas of the Secretariat (conference services, social development, women's equality, programme planning and evaluation). I not only knew of individuals, but had worked side by side with them.

My determination to ensure that women were fully represented at all levels originated with the goals of the UN and with being a founding member of the Group on Equal Rights for Women. I was also inspired by the leadership of Martti Ahtisaari, when he headed the UNTAG mission (Namibia) a few years earlier. For the first time in any UN mission, he placed women as regional office heads, and used international support staff ---mostly women --- on professional posts. Breaking with tradition, one of his appointments was our distinguished Special Adviser on Gender Issues and our Moderator, Rachel Mayanja, who on that mission, was the first woman to be appointed as Chief Liaison Officer with the Military—a non-traditional female assignment.

I also used my knowledge of individual women when inviting them to apply for the mission. Most did and felt it their most rewarding UN experience. I sometimes used the same knowledge to request men with experience or special skills, but men were far less shy of applying and getting posts in missions.

I believe that to date I am the only Chief of Mission who was also in Human Resources, and I used those resources to get the best. The mission rose form a handful to about 500. Later just before the elections in April 1994, we had over 2,000 working as election observers. We had to encourage interested people from outside the UN and permanent missions proved most helpful in supplying both men and women. The UN Volunteers also cooperated by supplying not only gender balance but many volunteers from Africa which was greatly appreciated by the local population.

In discussing strategies for increasing the number of women in UN peace operations in 2007 and beyond, we have to recognize that decentralization has increasingly shifted power from OHRM to DPKO and the Special

Representatives of the Secretary-General (SRSGs). In our annual assessments of the extent to which resolution 1325 has been implemented, the head of DPKO has consistently highlighted new developments and mechanisms, especially those for dealing with violence, exploitation and rape of local women and gender mainstreaming. I applaud the increase in the last two years of women serving in peace operations from 27.5 to 30%, somewhat higher that the increase in the Secretariat as a whole. Yet, I am appalled that following Carolyn McAskie's transfer after her outstanding leadership in Burundi and the resignation of Heidi Tagliavini in Georgia there is not a single woman SRSG. At the deputy level (DSRSG), there is only one woman, in Afghanistan.

I now wish to propose ten practical strategies which should accelerate the process of getting more women into peace operations:

• First, the incoming Secretary-General should appoint a woman with a gender-sensitive approach as the next Under-Secretary-General of the Department of Peacekeeping Operations;

• Second, a generic profile of a Secretary-General's Special Representative (SRSGs) or Head/Chief of Mission should be widely publicized and placed on the DPKO and Department of Political Affairs web sites;

• Third, a pool of at least 20 women should be selected for SRSG posts from the central high-level list kept by DPKO/OHRM and interviewed for suitability (language, managerial skills, region etc.).

• Fourth, a list of 5-8 of the 20 should be drawn up who are judged most suitable and who could be deployed at short notice (I believe that the new senior leadership policy unit in DPKO is scheduled to work on this aspect);

• Fifth, a letter from the Secretary-General or his Deputy should be sent to all Foreign Ministers, requesting women candidates for high-level civilian, military and police posts in peace operations;

• Sixth, no interviews or screening should be held unless a substantial number of women candidates (one third, at least) are included in the short list;

• Seventh, a search should be made of D-1 ad D-2 staff of UN agencies and bodies to ensure that women as well as men are chosen to head missions. To my knowledge only three women have ever been selected from UN bodies for DSRSG posts (Ethiopia/Eritrea, Guatemala and Afghanistan) whereas there is a double-digit figure for retiring D-2 male resident representatives/coordinator who have been selected as SRSGs or their deputies;

• Eighth, women Permanent Representatives should be considered and selected to head missions. Over the years, from an excellent and increasing pool of women Ambassadors accredited to UN offices in Addis Ababa,

Geneva, New York and Vienna, not a single one has been selected to head a mission whereas several of their male counterparts have;

• Ninth, DPKO's system for recruiting staff from within or outside the UN needs to be drastically revamped to fill the 21% vacancies rapidly and to take full advantage of women available to serve on mission;

• And tenth, if the DPKO Gender Adviser is to have any real access and influence on these selections, the post should be upgraded at least to the D-2/1 level.

May I say how heartened I am by the recent pronouncement by our Secretary-General designate, Mr. Ban Ki-Moon, that he was committed to having gender balance at the highest levels. He is also reported as saying that he was contemplating having a woman Deputy.

I would close by appealing to the new Secretary-General to extend his commitment to having women on high-level posts to peace operations also. I would then appeal to Member States to send more women candidates and to women staff to make themselves available for these exciting opportunities within the UN peace-keeping and peace-making operations.

GRAÇA MACHEL

Graça Machel
(nee Simbine)
3rd wife of Nelson mandela

B. 1945.

Matthew Cooper 2011

"Without the leadership exercised by Madam Graca Machel born from the personal hardship of a woman's experience with conflict, the world would not have placed the question of children in armed conflict on the international security and peace agendas. It is firmly there to stay."

— *Suzanne Mubarak*
First Lady of Egypt

§ A CHILDREN'S CHAMPION *

In 1994, Graça Machel's reputation as an educator and children's champion led United Nations Secretary-General Boutros Boutros-Ghali to name her the Expert in charge of producing a ground-breaking report on the impact of armed conflict on childrenl. The report was requested in late 1993 by the UN Committee on the Rights of the Child and the General Assembly. Ms. Machel served as Mozambique's first post-independence Minister for Education and within 10 years, school enrolment had doubled to over 80 per cent of school-age children. She continues to be active in reconstruction and development initiatives in Mozambique. She is President of the Foundation of Community Development and Chairperson of the National Organization of Children of Mozambique. She has worked closely with many UN organizations and

---

* Introduction to the Report on the impact of armed conflict on children (A/51/306), prepared by Ms. Graça Machel, the expert appointed by the UN Secretary-General, on 8 June 1994, pursuant to General Assembly resolution 48/157 of 20 December 1993.

was awarded the 1995 Nansen Medal in recognition of her outstanding contributions on behalf of refugee children. She is the widow of the country's first President, Samora Machel, killed in an airplane crash in 1986.

...

I am privileged to have been given the opportunity to report on a topic that I believe is of fundamental importance to humanity. In the past decade, 2 million children have been killed in armed conflict. Three times as many have been seriously injured or permanently disabled. Millions of others have been forced to witness or even take part in horrifying acts of violence. It is impossible to give accurate statistics on this carnage. The conservative estimates available hide the numbers of children whose murders are concealed and remain unrecorded, who are erased from the memory of humankind when whole families and communities are wiped out. Yet it is clear that increasingly, children are targets, not incidental casualties, of armed conflict.

I come from a culture where traditionally, children are seen as both our present and our future, so I have always believed it is our responsibility as adults to give children futures worth having. In the two years spent on this report, I have been shocked and angered to see how shamefully we have failed in this responsibility.

In some countries, conflicts have raged for so long that children have grown into adults without ever knowing peace. I have spoken to a child who was raped by soldiers when she was just nine years old. I have witnessed the anguish of a mother who saw her children blown to pieces by land-mines in their fields, just when she believed they had made it home safely after the war. I have listened to children forced to watch while their families were brutally slaughtered. I have heard the bitter remorse of 15-year-old ex-soldiers mourning their lost childhood and innocence, and I have been chilled listening to children who have been so manipulated by adults and so corrupted by their experiences of conflict that they could not recognize the evil of which they had been a part. These are the stories behind the figures given in this report — figures of such magnitude that they often hide the impact of these horrors on each child, each family, each community.

This report has given me the opportunity to learn about more than just the brutality of armed conflict, however. In Lebanon, I visited the site of an 'education for peace' project set up by children, with support from UNICEF. Where only months before there had been division, bitterness and hatred between communities, I found a group of teenagers interacting positively, exchanging experiences. These teenagers have managed to build bridges of communication where so many adults had failed. Hundreds of youth volunteers, many of them former militia members, have been mobilized as militants for peace. Those children understand that preventing the conflicts of tomorrow means changing the mind-set of youth today.

I have learned that despite being targets in contemporary armed conflicts, despite the brutality shown towards them and the failure of adults to nurture and protect them, children are both our reason to eliminate the worst aspects of armed conflict and our best hope of succeeding in that charge. In a disparate world, children are a unifying force capable of bringing us all together in support of a common ethic.

This was demonstrated repeatedly in the interactive, consultative process of research and mobilization that led to this report, involving all elements of civil society, and in particular, women and children, communities, academic institutions, non-governmental organizations (NGOs), UN agencies, governments and regional organizations.

In particular, six regional consultations were held: in Asia and the Pacific, Eastern and Southern Africa, Europe, Latin America, the Middle East, and West and Central Africa. Field visits were made to several areas affected by armed conflicts: Angola, Cambodia, Colombia, Northern Ireland, Lebanon, Rwanda (and refugee camps in Tanzania and Zaire), Sierra Leone and former Yugoslavia. There I met with officials and with children and their families to ensure that the final report reflects the immediate concerns of the people most directly affected. More than 20 thematic research papers and workshops were specially commissioned as background materials. The report greatly benefited from the input of a group of eminent persons including Belisario Betancur (Colombia), Francis Deng

(Sudan), Marian Wright Edelman (USA), Devaki Jain (India), Julius K. Nyerere (Tanzania), Lisbet Palme (Sweden), Wole Soyinka (Nigeria) and Archbishop Desmond Tutu (South Africa). Additional guidance came from a group of technical advisers representing diverse professional, political, religious and cultural backgrounds, and I received key support from the UN Centre for Human Rights, UNICEF and the Office of the UN High Commissioner for Refugees.

As a result, this report is undoubtedly a collaborative effort and only one part of a larger global movement to protect the rights of children as stated in the Convention on the Rights of the Child . The report is complementary to the work of the UN Committee on the Rights of the Child, NGOs and UN agencies working in the areas of human rights, humanitarian assistance and development, whose concern has helped create space for political and social mobilization at local, national and international levels.

Above all else, this process has strengthened my conviction that we must do anything and everything to protect children, to give them priority and a better future. This report is a call to action and a call to embrace a new morality that puts children where they belong — at the heart of all agendas. Protecting children from the impact of armed conflict is everyone's responsibility — governments, international organizations and every element of civil society. Therefore my challenge to each of you reading this report is that you ask yourself what you can do to make a difference. And then take that action, no matter how large or how small. For our children have a right to peace.

§ IMPACT OF ARMED CONFLICT ON CHILDREN

By Graça Machel *

Millions of children are caught up in conflicts in which they are not merely bystanders, but targets. Some fall victim to a general onslaught against civilians; others die as part of a calculated genocide. Still other children suffer the effects of sexual violence or the multiple deprivations of armed conflict that expose them to hunger or disease. Just as shocking, thousands of young people are cynically exploited as combatants.

In 1995, 30 major armed conflicts raged in different locations around the world. 1/ All of them took place

* Extracts from the ground-breaking Report on the impact of armed conflict on children (A/51/306). The Report, published on 26 August 1996, was undertaken with the support of the United Nations Centre for Human Rights and the United Nations Children's Fund, as provided for in the resolution, and is the fruit of extensive and wide-ranging consultations.

within States, between factions split along ethnic, religious or cultural lines. The conflicts destroyed crops, places of worship and schools. Nothing was spared, held sacred or protected - not children, families or communities. In the past decade, an estimated two million children have been killed in armed conflict. Three times as many have been seriously injured or permanently disabled, many of them maimed by landmines. 2/ Countless others have been forced to witness or even to take part in horrifying acts of violence.

These statistics are shocking enough, but more chilling is the conclusion to be drawn from them: more and more of the world is being sucked into a desolate moral vacuum. This is a space devoid of the most basic human values; a space in which children are slaughtered, raped, and maimed; a space in which children are exploited as soldiers; a space in which children are starved and exposed to extreme brutality. Such unregulated terror and violence speak of deliberate victimization. There are few further depths to which humanity can sink.

The lack of control and the sense of dislocation and chaos that characterize contemporary armed conflicts can be attributed to many different factors. Some observers point to cataclysmic political upheavals and struggles for control over resources in the face of widespread poverty and economic disarray. Others see the callousness of modern warfare as a natural outcome of the social revolutions that have torn traditional societies apart. The latter analysts point as proof to many African societies that have always had strong martial cultures. While fierce in battle, the rules and customs of those societies, only a few generations ago, made it taboo to attack women and children.

Whatever the causes of modern-day brutality towards children, the time has come to call a halt. The present report exposes the extent of the problem and proposes many practical ways to pull back from the brink. Its most fundamental demand is that children simply have no part in warfare. The international community must denounce this attack on children for what it is - intolerable and unacceptable.

Children can help. In a world of diversity and disparity, children are a unifying force capable of bringing people to common ethical grounds. Children's needs and aspirations cut across all ideologies and cultures. The needs of all children are the same: nutritious food, adequate health care, a decent education, shelter and a secure and loving family. Children are both our reason to struggle to eliminate the worst aspects of warfare, and our best hope for succeeding at it.

Concern for children has brought us to a common standard around which to rally. In the Convention on the Rights of the Child, the world has a unique instrument that almost every country has ratified. The single most important resolve that the world could make would be to transform universal ratification of this Convention into universal reality.

It was this challenge, of turning good intentions into real change for children, that led the United Nations Committee on the Rights of the Child in 1993 to recommend to the General Assembly, in accordance with article 45 (c)of the Convention on the Rights of the Child, that it request the Secretary- General to undertake a comprehensive study on the impact of armed conflict on children.

(...)

Violent conflict has always made victims of non-combatants. The patterns and characteristics of contemporary armed conflicts, however, have increased the risks for children. Vestiges of colonialism and persistent economic, social and political crises have greatly contributed to the disintegration of public order. Undermined by internal dissent, countries caught up in conflict today are also under severe stress from a global world economy that pushes them ever further towards the margins. Rigorous programmes of structural adjustment promise long-term market-based economic growth, but demands for immediate cuts in budget deficits and public expenditure only weaken already fragile States, leaving them dependent on forces and relations over which they have little control. While many developing countries have made considerable economic progress in recent decades, the benefits have often been spread unevenly, leaving millions of people struggling for survival. The collapse of functional Governments in many countries torn by internal fighting and the erosion of essential service structures have fomented inequalities, grievances and strife. The personalization of power and leadership and the manipulation of ethnicity and religion to serve personal or narrow group interests have had similarly debilitating effects on countries in conflict.

All of these elements have contributed to conflicts, between Governments and rebels, between different opposition groups vying for supremacy and among populations at large, in struggles that take the form of widespread civil unrest. Many drag on for long periods with no clear beginning or end, subjecting successive generations to endless struggles for survival.

Distinctions between combatants and civilians disappear in battles fought from village to village or from street to street. In recent decades, the proportion of war victims who are civilians has leaped dramatically from 5 per cent to over 90 per cent. The struggles that claim more civilians than soldiers have been marked by horrific levels of violence and brutality. Any and all tactics are employed, from systematic rape, to scorched-earth tactics that destroy crops and poison wells, to ethnic cleansing and genocide. With all standards abandoned, human rights violations against children and women occur in unprecedented numbers. Increasingly, children have become the targets and even the perpetrators of violence and atrocities.

Children seek protection in networks of social support, but these have been undermined by new political and economic realities. Conflict and violent social change have affected social welfare networks between families and communities. Rapid urbanization and the spread of market-based values have also helped erode systems of support that were once based on the extended family.

Unbridled attacks on civilians and rural communities have provoked mass exoduses and the displacement of entire populations who flee conflict in search of elusive sanctuaries within and outside their national borders. Among these uprooted millions, it is estimated that 80 per cent are children and women.

Involving children as soldiers has been made easier by the proliferation of inexpensive light weapons. Previously, the more dangerous weapons were either heavy or complex, but these guns are so light that children can use them and so simple that they can be stripped and reassembled by a child of 10. The international arms trade has made assault rifles cheap and widely available so the poorest communities now have access to deadly weapons capable of transforming any local conflict into a bloody slaughter. In Uganda, an AK-47 automatic machine gun can be purchased for the cost of a chicken and, in northern Kenya, it can be bought for the price of a goat.

Moreover, the rapid spread of information today has changed the character of modern warfare in important ways. While the world surely benefits from ready access to information, it will pay a price if it fails to recognize that information is never entirely neutral. International media are frequently influenced by one or another of the parties to a conflict, by commercial realities and by the public's degree of interest in humanitarian action. The result of these influences are depictions that can be selective or uneven, or both. Whether a story is reported or not may depend less on its intrinsic importance than on subjective perceptions of the public's appetite for information and on the expense of informing them. For example, while coverage of the conflicts in Bosnia and Herzegovina and Somalia was extensive, very little has been reported about the conflicts in Afghanistan and Angola. The media is capable of effectively galvanizing international public support for humanitarian action, as it did for Indo-Chinese refugees in the late 1970s and for Somalia in 1992. The threat of adverse international publicity may also be positive, holding the potential for keeping some gross violations of human rights in check. Ultimately, however, while reports of starving children or overcrowded camps for displaced persons may be dramatic, they do little to support efforts for long-term reconstruction and reconciliation.

(...)

Armed conflicts across and between communities result in massive levels of destruction; physical, human, moral and cultural. Not only are large numbers of children killed and injured, but countless others grow up deprived of their material and emotional needs, including the structures that give meaning to social and cultural life. The entire fabric of their societies - their homes, schools, health systems and religious institutions - are torn to pieces.

War violates every right of a child - the right to life, the right to be with family and community, the right to health, the right to the development of the personality and the right to be nurtured and protected. Many of today's conflicts last the length of a "childhood", meaning that from birth to early adulthood, children will experience multiple and accumulative assaults. Disrupting the social networks and primary relationships that support children's physical, emotional, moral, cognitive and social development in this way, and for this duration, can have profound physical and psychological implications.

In countless cases, the impact of armed conflict on children's lives remains invisible. The origin of the problems of many children who have been affected by conflicts is obscured. The children themselves may be removed from the public, living in institutions or, as is true of thousands of unaccompanied and orphaned children, exist as street children or become victims of prostitution. Children who have lost parents often experience humiliation, rejection and discrimination. For years, they may suffer in silence as their self-esteem crumbles away. Their insecurity and fear cannot be measured.

(...)

One of the most alarming trends in armed conflict is the participation of children as soldiers. Children serve armies in supporting roles, as cooks, porters, messengers and spies. Increasingly, however, adults are deliberately conscripting children as soldiers. Some commanders have even noted the desirability of child soldiers because they are "more obedient, do not question orders and are easier to manipulate than adult soldiers".

A series of 24 case studies on the use of children as soldiers prepared for the present report, covering conflicts over the past 30 years, indicate that government or rebel armies around the world have recruited tens of thousands of children. Most are adolescents, though many child soldiers are 10 years of age or younger. While the majority are boys, girls also are recruited. The children most likely to become soldiers are those from impoverished and marginalized backgrounds and those who have become separated from their families.

(...)

The present report has set forth recommendations for the protection of children during armed conflict. It has concentrated on what is practical and what is possible, but this cannot be enough. In considering the future of children, we must be daring. We must look beyond what seems immediately possible and find new ways and new solutions to shield children from the consequences of war and to directly address the conflicts themselves.

There is a clear and overwhelming moral case for protecting all children while seeking the peaceful resolution of wars and challenging the justification for any armed conflict. That children are still being so shamefully abused is a clear indication that we have barely begun to fulfill our obligations to protect them. The immediate wounds to children, the physical injury, the sexual violence, the psychosocial distress, are affronts to each and every humanitarian impulse that inspired the Convention on the Rights of the Child. The Convention commits States to meet a much broader range of children's rights, to fulfill the rights to health, to education and to growth and development within caring and supportive families and communities.

The report has shown how all rights to which children are entitled are consistently abused during armed conflict. Throwing a spotlight on such abuses is one small step towards addressing them. Exposure challenges perpetrators to face up to their actions and reminds defenders of children's rights of the enormity of the task ahead. The only measure by which the present report can be judged is the response it draws and the action it stimulates. To some extent, both are already under way: the report has in many ways broken new ground, focusing not just on the debate or resolution that form the final product, but on a process of consultation and cooperation among Governments, international agencies, NGOs and many other elements of civil society. Above all, the report has engaged families and children in explaining their situations and asserting their rights.

The present report's mobilization work is ongoing. Commitments have already been made, at national and regional levels, to hold meetings that will begin to implement the report's conclusions. Further publications are planned, including a book, a series of research papers, information kits and a popular version of the report. In the preparation of the report, there were many other issues that could not be covered in the time available, and that demand further investigation. These include: operational issues affecting the protection of children in emergencies; child-centred approaches to the prevention of conflict and to reconstruction and development; the treatment of child rights violations within existing human rights mechanisms; the role of the military in protecting child rights; child rights issues in relation to peace and security agendas; special programming for adolescents in conflict situations, and particularly child-headed households; the role of women in conflict prevention, management and resolution; community and regional approaches to humanitarian relief; and the development of effective training programmes in the area of child rights for all actors in conflict situations. In following up the present report, it is recommended that each of these issues be pursued through research and other means.

The flagrant abuse and exploitation of children during armed conflict can and must be eliminated. For too long, we have given ground to spurious claims that the involvement of children in armed conflict is regrettable but inevitable. It is not. Children are regularly caught up in warfare as a result of conscious and deliberate decisions made by adults. We must challenge each of these decisions and we must refute the flawed political and military reasoning, the protests of impotence, and the cynical attempts to disguise child soldiers as merely the youngest "volunteers".

Above all else, the present report is a call to action. It is unconscionable that we so clearly and consistently see children's rights attacked and that we fail to defend them. It is unforgivable that children are assaulted, violated, murdered and yet our conscience is not revolted nor our sense of dignity challenged. This represents a fundamental crisis of our civilization. The impact of armed conflict on children must be everyone's concern and is everyone's responsibility; Governments, international organizations and every element of civil society. Each one of us, each individual, each institution, each country, must initiate and support global action to protect children. Local and national strategies must strengthen and be strengthened through international mobilization.

Let us claim children as "zones of peace". In this way, humankind will finally declare that childhood is inviolate and that all children must be spared the pernicious effects of armed conflict. Children present us with a uniquely compelling motivation for mobilization. Universal concern for children presents new opportunities to confront the problems that cause their suffering. By focusing on children, politicians, Governments, the military and non-

State entities will begin to recognize how much they destroy through armed conflict and, therefore, how little they gain. Let us take this opportunity to recapture our instinct to nourish and protect children. Let us transform our moral outrage into concrete action. Our children have a right to peace. Peace is every child's right.

§ THE PLIGHT OF CHILDREN

By Graça Machel *

It is with deep appreciation that I have come from Africa to receive the honour of the North-South Prize.

The Award is a tribute to all those who have worked with me to focus international attention on the plight of the world's children.

It is an endorsement of all those who are seeking to ensure that the world acts to redress the plight of children.

Above all it gives recognition to the courage of the children themselves. They have taught us how painfully far

* Excerpts from Graça Machel speech on accepting the Council of Europe's North-South prize, Strasbourg, 28 January 1999.

we still are from according to the most vulnerable of humans the rights by which we define humanity.

I would also like to say how much I appreciate sharing the Prize with Lloyd Axworthy, who has made such an effective contribution to the campaign to rid the world of landmines.

The honour is all the greater because the Council of Europe represents a great part of the industrialised world, and the Prize expresses a commitment on the part of Europe to work with countries of the South for a new relationship. Central to that new relationship must be a partnership to correct the historic imbalances between the richer and the poorer parts of the world, the weaker and the more powerful.

By using this Prize to highlight the scourge of land mines and the state of the world's children, as well as the needs of development, you are encouraging concrete action to build this partnership.

You are declaring in the most practical way that Europe is part of the world's response to the greatest challenge facing humanity as the new millennium approaches.

When the Council of Europe was founded in defence of human rights and democracy, it formed part of a new international order. Those who established that order wished to prevent the repetition of the economic crises, destructive wars, and violation of human rights that Europe in particular had witnessed.

Fifty years later we are all challenged by the fact that millions across the globe live in impoverished and insecure conditions that prevent them from exercising the rights that have been proclaimed to be universal.

This is especially and shockingly true of children.

Although the problems are especially acute in the developing world, it is not only in the developing world that children are afflicted by the violence of poverty. The problem is a global one.

We have come to understand the scale of the horror better, thanks to the work of many international and national agencies. But the statistics still have the capacity to shock us, and rightly so. With your permission I will recall a few.

The focus of my own work has brought home to me the impact of armed conflict on children. Amongst other things:

* million children have been killed and 4,5 million have been wounded in wars in the past decade. Still more have been left homeless; orphaned; traumatized, not to speak of those who are raped;

* Increasing numbers of children under 16, an estimated 300,000, have become involved in armed conflict as child soldiers.

When one looks more broadly at the condition of children one sees the justification of speaking of the violence of poverty:

* The "silent emergency" of malnutrition and preventable disease kills 12 million children each year;

* Over 70 million children between 10 and 14 years are employed in child labour;

* Millions have no home or family.

Today we are also becoming aware of the devastating impact that HIV/AIDS has on children. All too often we think of this mainly as an adult problem. I must acknowledge that I myself have only recently understood the extent to which children are affected:

* In sub-Saharan Africa, which has borne the brunt of this disease, AIDS has by now orphaned an estimated 8 million children.

I am aware that one of the criteria for receiving the North-South Prize is "the demonstration of clear hope for the future of human rights protection". But I think all of us will acknowledge that at times it is not easy to speak about the suffering of children without feeling tempted to despair.

What leads us in this direction is an apparent discrepancy between our principles and our practice where children are concerned.

After all, the modern world economy has the capacity to produce more than enough to meet their needs.

And the international community has developed an unprecedented array of institutions, policies and declarations that proclaim the rights of children and other vulnerable groups. There is a host of conventions, treaties and other instruments that guarantee those rights and entrench them.

And yet in many respects the situation of children has worsened. This is not to ignore or devalue the significant advances and improvements that have been made. Nor is it a counsel of despair. But we cannot escape the contradiction between what, as an international community, we have proclaimed ought to happen and the preventable wrongs that happen in reality.

It is for that reason that we are led to speak of a moral crisis in humanity.

The recent world economic crisis has shown yet again that although we are a single, interdependent, world in which none can escape the effects of such crises, the burden falls most heavily on the developing countries and on their peoples. And everything that we have learnt tells us that it is the children who will be feeling the harshest and the most permanent effects.

Can we therefore claim in all earnestness to love our children - the children of the North and the South - if we do not also give the most serious attention to preventing our world, which has more than enough resources, from dividing ever more deeply between rich and poor!

Can we speak sincerely of peace and allow the cynical exploitation of children as soldiers to continue! We must bring it to an end, whether it is facilitated by the spread in far away countries of light weapons mainly manufactured in the North, or by the failure of the international community to raise the age of recruitment to 18!

Can we speak of effective international norms of justice until the International Criminal Court is fully empowered to deal with atrocities committed against children and women!

I believe that the Council of Europe does give us some reason to think that it is possible to hope for a better future for children.

In establishing a North-South Centre; in choosing to associate its fiftieth anniversary celebrations with action for global solidarity and the eradication of poverty; in choosing Africa as the principal focus of its relations with the South, the Council bears witness to a mobilisation in Europe to help realise our shared vision of a better world.

We also take note that it was under the Portuguese Presidency of the Security Council that the relevance of the violations of child rights for international peace and security gained new recognition. This has created important opportunities to improve standards for the protection of children, to strengthen humanitarian assistance and to mobilise resources towards these ends.

However hopes have too often been confounded for us to be complacent. Too often, resolution to redress distant wrongs has been blunted by the urgency of more immediate interests.

What is required is determined, concerted and sustained action by the nations of the world in a partnership of industrialised and developing countries, and between governments and their peoples.

By paying tribute to those who work to make the world a better place for our children, you are helping to put these issues high on the agenda of one of the most powerful associations of nations as it renews its relationship with the developing world.

ELEANOR ROOSEVELT

Matthew Couper
Eleanor Roosevelt
2011
Pencil on paper
7" x 5" / 175mm x 135mm
www.mattcouper.com

(Anna) Eleanor Roosevelt

... co founder of the 'Freedom House'
... was a U.N.-chaired committee that
drafted 'Universal Declaration of Human Rights'

Matthew Coope 2011

"*Eleanor Roosevelt was one of the most influential figures of the 20th century, and her life spanned some of the most dramatic and challenging events in modern history. Steadfast in her commitment to America, democracy, and a world that honored human rights, she told Americans across the Nation, 'We are on trial to show what democracy means.'*"

— Bill Clinton
Former US President (1993-2001)

§ THE FIRST LADY OF HUMAN RIGHS

By Allida M. Black *

When during World War II Eleanor Roosevelt dared to equate American racism with fascism and argued that to ignore the evils of segregation would be capitulating to Aryanism, hostility toward her reached an all-time high. Newspapers from Chicago to Louisiana covered the dispute and numerous citizens pleaded with J. Edgar Hoover, Director of the FBI, to silence her. Refusing to concede to her opponents, she continuously asserted that if the nation continued to honor Jim Crow, America would have defeated fascism abroad only to defend racism at home.

* Allida M. Black, PhD, is Project Director and Editor of The Eleanor Roosevelt Papers, a project designed to preserve, teach and apply Eleanor Roosevelt's writings and discussions of human rights and democratic politics, and Research Professor of History and International Affairs at The George Washington University. Courtesy of The Eleanor Roosevelt Papers.

Eleanor Roosevelt said the same things in private that she did in public. Whether interceding with the president for Walter White, Mary McLeod Bethune, A. Philip Randolph, or W.E.B. DuBois; raising money for Howard University or Bethune-Cookman College; investigating discrimination black women encountered while stationed at the Women's Auxiliary Army Corps base in Des Moines, Iowa; pressing the Fair Employment Practices Commission to investigate complaints; or supporting anti-segregation campaigns and anti-lynching legislation, ER pressed to keep civil rights issues on the top of the domestic political agenda. Consequently, throughout the war years, her standing with civil rights leaders increased while her standing with some key White House aides decreased.

While the advent of World War II reinforced ER's commitment to the New Deal and social reform, it also allowed her to expand the scope of her activities at home and abroad. Even before the war began, concern for the plight of European refugees fueled her work with such groups as the Emergency Rescue Committee and the U.S. Committee for the Care of European Children. She also helped Varian Fry in his efforts to aid Jews escaping Nazi-occupied Europe. At the same time, ER responded to many individual appeals for help but stringent U.S. immigration laws restricted her efforts. In an unsuccessful effort to change the laws, ER lobbied Congress particularly on behalf of the Child Refugee Bill which would have allowed an additional 10,000 children a year above the German quota to enter the United States over a two-year period.

Once the war began in December 1941, she continued to aid individual refugees, work with organized groups and did not hesitate to criticize the State Department's interpretation of the immigration laws, especially the obstructionist position of visa operations chief Breckinridge Long. She did have allies within the department, however, most notably Assistant Secretary of State Sumner Welles with whom she worked closely to secure additional entrance visas. Still, ER would have been the first to admit that she never achieved all she hoped for in the cause of refugee relief and resettlement.

On the home front, ER wanted Americans to learn from the mistakes of World War I and win both the war and the peace that would follow. To that end, she did all she could do to promote democracy and maintain civilian morale in a variety of different venues. For example, she actively urged women to work out outside the home, particularly in defense industries, and lobbied to have day care centers and take-out kitchens built in factories. She also strongly supported equal pay for equal work. She encouraged volunteerism generally and even served briefly as deputy director of the Office of Civilian Defense until Congressional criticism over alleged favoritism and boondoggling forced her resignation in February 1942. Mindful of the continuing discrimination against African Americans she played an important role in the establishment of the Fair Employment Practices Commission which outlawed discrimination in industries that received defense contracts and helped ensure that African American units such as the Tuskegee Airmen participated in combat operations.

Nor did ER neglect the military. She was a strong supporter of the new women's military services and the armed forces in general. She corresponded with several individual soldiers and worked to address their concerns. She helped soften the tone of FDR's standard condolence letter to the families of military personnel killed in action and used her column to place the GIs' concerns before Congress and the public. ER also toured military installations at home and abroad. She made extensive visits to both the European and Pacific Theatres where she visited military hospitals, ate in the mess halls and in one case walked down a road to say good by and good luck to truckloads of men on their way to the battlefront.

ER angered some White House aides by her insistent demand that New Deal reforms continue during wartime. Vowing that she would not put the New Deal away in storage, ER pressured FDR's aides, liberal leaders, and concerned Americans to remember that there was an economic emergency in addition to a military one. Thus, by the 1944 presidential election, the two camps within the Roosevelt Administration became even more clearly defined.

This division became apparent as the campaign got under way. ER and FDR's conservative campaign manager, Robert Hannegan, opposed each other. She thought he was too focused on winning at the expense of issues she considered important while he resented her support of Henry Wallace and her activism on behalf of African Americans. Consequently ER was less influential in Democratic party councils than she had been in previous presidential elections. Publicly she campaigned in a non-partisan fashion----what she described as "making non-political speeches about registering and voting" and used her column to discuss such political issues as full employment and housing without referring to the campaign. Behind the scenes she also encouraged FDR to take a more active role in campaigning especially after his poll numbers dropped in September 1944. Once FDR was elected in November, she urged him to keep domestic matters at the top of his agenda, telling the president and his aide Harry Hopkins, that they were "under moral obligation to see his domestic reforms through, particularly the organizing of our domestic life in such a way as to give everybody a job."

When FDR died April 12 1945, ER was well prepared personally and politically for the challenges facing her. She had close confidants, colleagues, and friends to turn to for support. And, although she was hurt to find that Mercer had been with FDR when he suffered a fatal stroke, she quickly recovered and resumed her commitments.

The question ER faced in 1945 was what her public role would be. Invitations poured into the White House, her apartment in New York City, and her home at Val-Kill. Now that she was no longer First Lady, Eleanor Roosevelt was anxious to leave the White House. Within a week of FDR's death, she had coordinated his funeral, responded to friends' condolences, overseen the boxing of possessions acquired and documents generated during her twelve years in Washington, said goodbye to colleagues and staff, and pondered her future. Despite the intensity of this schedule, ER made time April 19th to host a farewell White House tea for the women's press corps. Although the reception was a private affair, ER did answer some questions for the record. After scoffing at various rumors of her own political ambitions, ER declared that her only aspirations were journalistic ones. The next evening after arriving in Manhattan, she faced those questions for a second time. Confronted by a small group of photographers and reporters outside her Washington Square apartment, ER refused to comment on their speculations. "The story," she said, "is over."

Despite these denials, politicians, pundits and the public openly speculated on what actions Eleanor Roosevelt should take next. Speaker of the House Sam Rayburn and New Jersey Congresswoman Mary Norton urged ER to join the American delegation to the conference charged with planning the United Nations. Secretary of the Interior Harold Ickes pleaded with her to run for the United States Senate while New York Democratic party leader Ed Flynn argued that she should be the Empire State's next governor. Others proposed that she be the new Secretary of Labor. Even the syndicated columnists Joseph and Stewart Alsop belatedly joined the conjecture, satirically suggesting that their cousin become Truman's new political "medium."

Close friends and the media reinforced this expectation. As they rode the train from FDR's Hyde Park funeral back to Washington, Henry Morgenthau Jr. recommended that FDR's estate be settled as soon as possible so she could speak out to the world, arguing that it was most important that her voice be heard. After encouraging her friend to take a brief rest, Hickok reminded ER that she was independent now, freer than she had ever been before, and that "a very important place awaited" her. The Associated Press agreed, succinctly summarizing the pressures confronting ER with this front page headline: "Mrs. Roosevelt Will Continue Column; Seeks No Office *Now*."

Eleanor Roosevelt had her own expectations about the future; however, unlike her friends and the media, she was undecided about what actions she should take to achieve them. Fearing that her public life died along with FDR, Eleanor Roosevelt struggled to set her own course. Although she declared her determination not to continually be seen as a former First Lady, ER feared that without the ear of the president she would lose the influence she struggled so diligently to attain. At times she succumbed to these anxieties only to encounter jocular criticism from those closest to her. When a self-pitying ER informed young friends that she merely wanted to write, visit her family, and live a peaceful life, Trude Lash teasingly suggested that they all go buy ER a lace cap as a retirement gift.

But as ER reflected on her life, she drew confidence from the way that she had handled previous political expectations. In New York, she had managed her career as teacher, journalist, and political organizer without discounting her responsibilities as the Empire State's first lady. In the White House, she revolutionized the role of First

Lady by constantly acting in ways that were new to the position. She was the first (and only) First Lady to hold regular press conferences, write a daily newspaper column, publish books and articles, travel the nation on speaking tours, chair national conferences in the White House, address national conventions of social reform organizations, give a keynote address at her party's presidential convention, represent her nation abroad, travel battlefields, and direct a government agency. Clearly, she had numerous skills which could be applied to politics outside the White House.

Yet these new boundaries did not mean that new politics would follow. Eleanor Roosevelt had no plans to forsake the goals and ideals of the New Deal. In fact, she planned to do the exact opposite. If FDR had abandoned Dr. New Deal to become Dr. Win the War and resented her insistent wartime references to domestic problems, ER anticipated that his successor would be even less likely to pursue the controversial reforms FDR had postponed. She recognized that if the New Deal was to re-enter the political arena, she would have to assist in orchestrating its return. Whether she did this by promoting candidates or policy was up to her. The path she selected was not the pivotal point in her strategy. What was important was that she select a mode of operation which allowed her the greatest leeway in pursuing her own goals while she protected her husband's legacy.

For the next seventeen years of her life, until her death November 7, 1962, Eleanor Roosevelt carefully walked this line. She published *This I Remember*, her memoirs of her years in the White House. She gladly lent her name to Democratic Party fundraisers, campaigned for local, state and national candidates, and hosted events commemorating FDR's major accomplishments.

But it is her efforts as a politician in her own right that make her post White House years so unique. In December 1945, Harry Truman appointed her to the United States delegation to the United Nation where she stunned delegates with her political finesse she displayed in overseeing the drafting and unanimous passage of the Universal Declaration of Human Rights.

Although some of her colleagues on the U.S. delegation were initially skeptical of her appointment, ER soon won them over with her political acumen and diplomatic skill. Future secretary of state Dean Rusk who then headed the State Department's Office of Special Political Affairs described her and another future secretary of state John Foster Dulles as "the two best vote getters we had. Somehow finding room in their schedules, they met and worked hard on every delegate. In those years (they) produced overwhelming majorities on almost anything we wanted in the General Assembly." Even the Soviets with whom she often clashed respected her skill and tenacity in argument.

Ironically ER's initial assignment to the UN's Social, Humanitarian and Cultural Committee which was considered "safe" turned out to be the most contentious because the group dealt with an early Cold War issue: repatriation of displaced people, particularly those who feared return to the countries of origin because of their political views. In the committee and before the General Assembly, ER refuted the Soviet contention that these people were traitors or collaborators and argued that they should not be forced to return home. Each time the Soviet recommendations were voted down by sizeable margins and ultimately the UN and its subsidiary agency, the International Refugee Organization, came down in favor of resettlement rather than repatriation.

Important as her work on refugee issues was, ER's efforts on behalf of the Universal Declaration of Human Rights (UDHR) have had the greatest long-term impact. As chair of the subcommittee that drafted the UDHR she played a critical role in the creation of the declaration skillfully creating an atmosphere that permitted blending the ideas and norms of different cultures together in a document nations around the globe could assent to while marshaling U.S. support for swift passage of the declaration by separating it from a legally binding (and more problematic) covenant . Later as chairman of the Human Rights Commission, she presented the document to the General Assembly and was instrumental in its passage. Today, more than 50 years after its passage, the UDHR remains the touchstone of the global Human Rights movement and a key component of an international system that provides for international scrutiny of the way in which a nation treats its citizens.

While conscious of her role and responsibilities as a member of the American delegation, ER rarely hesitated to disagree with the government position especially when she felt the U.S. was not showing enough moral or political leadership on international issues. As a strong supporter of a Jewish homeland in Palestine, she openly criticized President Truman when he withdrew his support for the UN partition plan in favor of a plan to place Palestine under a temporary international trusteeship. In a letter to Secretary Marshall, ER argued that the decision "more or less buried the UN. I can hardly see how it can recover and have the slightest influence, since we are the only ones who could give it any force and we now have been the ones to take it away." Taking her argument public, she told readers of My Day, "We have taken the weak course of sacrificing the word we pledged and, in so doing, have weakened the UN and prevented it from becoming an instrument to keep peace in world."

At the same time she balanced the requirements of her position as an instructed delegate and the dictates of her own conscience especially on issues of civil rights for African Americans and other peoples of color. She ardently supported independence for people seeking to free themselves from colonial rule as well as for those behind the Iron Curtain, and she was tireless in her efforts to foster good relationships with newly-independent nations who wished to remain unaligned with either the Eastern or the Western bloc.

ER was equally indefatigable in her support of the United Nations calling it "the one hope" for peace. During and after her seven years as a delegate, she traveled extensively abroad investigating social, economic and political conditions in Europe, Asia, the Middle East and the Pacific. Everywhere she went she urged support for the UN and its humanitarian and diplomatic aid. At home she campaigned vigorously for the UN via "My Day," books and articles and, after 1952, traveled the country as a volunteer for the American Association of the United Nations.

Worried that FDR's death had deprived liberals of the leadership they needed to make America a more just democracy, ER pressured Democratic officials and liberal leaders to practice what they preached. Comfortable with her own power, ER remained uncomfortable with both consensus liberals and communist-front sympathizers. She remained dissatisfied with Truman, and he entered the election of 1948 without her endorsement. Yet as disappointed as she was with the Democratic Party in 1948, she refused to abandon the Democrats to promote a third party unsure of its membership or its principles.

The early postwar years were a difficult time for ER and for the country. Both were grappling with the consequences of unforeseen circumstances of FDR's sudden death and the problems inherent in converting from a wartime economy to a peacetime economy. Housing shortages, inflation and labor strikes dominated the headlines. At the same time, the reform spirit of the New Deal was dissipating as a more conservative spirit took hold in Congress and the nation at large. No longer tied to FDR's needs, ER became increasingly vocal on these and other social and economic issues such as health care and education especially when it became apparent that the Truman Administration lacked the will and the ability to resolve them. Her principal vehicle for communicating her views remained My Day but she also did not hesitate to confront Truman personally when she felt it was necessary.

Two themes consistently pervaded her activism during this period. One was that America's future security depended on a sound economy that promised jobs to all who wanted to work and a healthy, well-educated citizenry committed to the principles of democracy and equality. The other was America's emerging role as international leader. In her mind the two were linked. In September 1945, she asked readers of My Day, "The eyes of the world are on this nation. How can we expect the nations of the world to sit down together and solve their problems without war if we do not use the same mechanism to successfully in settling our domestic problems?"

Among the issues ER championed in the early postwar years were the continuation of wage and price controls, full employment legislation and national health insurance. She also backed labor's demands for increases in wages, supported its National Citizens Political Action Committee (NCPAC) and served as honorary co-chair of a committee to raise funds for striking workers. At the same time, she opposed the Taft-Hartley anti-union bill calling it "a bad bill" and advised Truman that the Democrats could not "out conserve the Republicans" and expect to be re-elected.

During this period ER also intensified her activism on behalf of civil rights speaking out more insistently in favor of anti-lynching legislation and an end to the poll tax. She also called for desegregation in housing, education, and other public facilities as well equal opportunities in employment and housing. She supported legislation to make the Fair Employment Practices Commission permanent and argued for the establishment of a Civil Rights Division within the Department of Justice.

§ THE STRUGGLE FOR HUMAN RIGHTS

By Eleanor Roosevelt *

I have come this evening to talk with you on one of the greatest issues of our time—that is the preservation of human freedom. I have chosen to discuss it here in France, at the Sorbonne, because here in this soil the roots of human freedom have long ago struck deep and here they have been richly nourished. It was here the Declaration of the Rights of Man was proclaimed, and the great slogans of the French Revolution--liberty, equality, fraternity--fired the imagination of men. I have chosen to discuss this issue in Europe because this has been the scene of the greatest historic battles between freedom and tyranny. I have chosen to discuss it in the early days of the General Assembly because the issue of human liberty is decisive for the settlement of outstanding political

---

* Speech to the Sorbonne University, Paris, September 28, 1948.

differences and for the future of the United Nations.

The decisive importance of this issue was fully recognized by the founders of the United Nations at San Francisco. Concern for the preservation and promotion of human rights and fundamental freedoms stands at the heart of the United Nations. Its Charter is distinguished by its preoccupation with the rights and welfare of individual men and women. The United Nations has made it clear that it intends to uphold human rights and to protect the dignity of the human personality. In the preamble to the Charter the keynote is set when it declares: "We the people of the United Nations determined...to reaffirm faith in fundamental human rights, in the dignity and worth of the human person, in the equal rights of men and women and of nations large and small, and ... to promote social progress and better standards of life in larger freedom." This reflects the basic premise of the Charter that the peace and security of mankind are dependent on mutual respect for the rights and freedoms of all.

One of the purposes of the United Nations is declared in article 1 to be: "to achieve international cooperation in solving international problems of an economic, social, cultural, or humanitarian character, and in promoting and encouraging respect for human rights and for fundamental freedoms for all without distinction as to race, sex, language, or religion."

This thought is repeated at several points and notably in articles 55 and 56 the Members pledge themselves to take joint and separate action in cooperation with the United

Nations for the promotion of "universal respect for, and observance of, human rights and fundamental freedoms for all without distinction as to race, sex, language, or religion."

The Human Rights Commission was given as its first and most important task the preparation of an International Bill of Rights. The General Assembly which opened its third session here in Paris a few days ago will have before it the first fruit of the Commissions's labors in this task, that is the International Declaration of Human Rights.

This Declaration was finally completed after much work during the last session of the Human Rights Commission in New York in the spring of 1948. The Economic and Social Council has sent it without recommendation to the General Assembly, together with other documents transmitted by the Human Rights Commission.

It was decided in our Commission that a Bill of Rights should contain two parts:

1. A Declaration which could be approved through action of the Member States of the United Nations in the General Assembly. This Declaration would have great moral force, and would say to the peoples of the world "this is what we hope human rights may mean to all people in the years to come." We have put down here the rights that we consider basic for individual human beings the world over to have. Without them, we feel that the full development of individual personality is impossible.

2. The second part of the bill, which the Human Rights Commission has not yet completed because of the lack of time, is a covenant which would be in the form of a treaty to be presented to the nations of the world. Each nation, as it is prepared to do so, would ratify this covenant and the covenant would then become binding on the nations which adhere to it. Each nation ratifying would then be obligated to change its laws wherever they did not conform to the points contained in the covenant.

This covenant, of course, would have to be a simpler document. It could not state aspirations, which we feel to be permissible in the Declaration. It could only state rights which could be assured by law and it must contain methods of implementation, and no state ratifying the covenant could be allowed to disregard it. The methods of implementation have not yet been agreed upon, nor have they been given adequate consideration by the Commission at any of its meetings. There certainly should be discussion on the entire question of this world Bill of Human Rights and there may be acceptance by this Assembly of the Declaration if they come to agreement on it. The acceptance of the Declaration, I think, should encourage every nation in the coming months to discuss its meaning with its people so that they will be better prepared to accept the covenant with a deeper understanding of the problems involved when that is presented, we hope, a year from now and, we hope, accepted.

The Declaration has come from the Human Rights Commission with unanimous acceptance except for four abstentions—the U.S.S.R., Yugoslavia, Ukraine, and Byelorussia. The reason for this is a fundamental difference in the conception of human rights as they exist in these states and in certain other Member States in the United Nations.

In the discussion before the Assembly, I think it should be made crystal clear what these differences are and tonight I want to spend a little time making them clear to you. It seems to me there is a valid reason for taking the time today to think carefully and clearly on the subject if human rights, because in the acceptance and observance of these rights lies the root, I believe, of our chance for peace in the future, and for the strengthening of the United Nations organization to the point where it can maintain peace in the future.

We must not be confused about what freedom is. Basic human rights are simple and easily understood: freedom of speech and a free press; freedom of religion and worship; freedom of assembly and the right of petition; the right of men to be secure in their homes and free from unreasonable search and seizure and from arbitrary arrest and punishment.

We must not be deluded by the efforts of the forces of reaction to prostitute the great words of our free tradition and thereby to confuse the struggle. Democracy, freedom, human rights have come to have a definite meaning to the people of the world which we must not allow any nation to so change that they are made synonymous with suppression and dictatorship.

There are basic differences that show up even in the use of words between a democratic and a totalitarian country. For instance "democracy" means one thing to the U.S.S.R. and another to the U.S.A. and, I know, in France. I have served since the first meeting of the nuclear commission on the Human Rights Commission, and I think this point stands out clearly.

The U.S.S.R. Representatives assert that they already have achieved many things which we, in what they call the "bourgeois democracies" cannot achieve because their government controls the accomplishment of these things. Our government seems powerless to them because, in the last analysis, it is controlled by the people. They would not put it that way - they would say that the people in the U.S.S.R. control their government by allowing their government to have certain absolute rights. We, on the other hand, feel that certain rights can never be granted to the government, but must be kept in the hands of the people.

For instance, the U.S.S.R. will assert that their press is free because the state makes it free by providing the machinery, the paper, and even the money for the salaries for the people who work on the paper. They state that there is no control over what is printed in the various papers that they subsidize in this manner, such, for instance, as a trade-union paper. But what would happen if a paper were to print ideas which were critical of the basic policies and beliefs of the Communist government? I am sure some good reason would be found for abolishing that paper.

It is true that there have been many cases where newspapers in the U.S.S.R. have criticized officials and their actions and have been responsible for the removal of those officials, but in doing so they did not criticize anything which was fundamental to Communist beliefs. They simply criticized methods of doing things, so one must differentiate between things which are permissible, such as criticism of any individual or of the manner of doing things, and the criticism of a belief which would be considered vital to the acceptance of Communism.

What are the differences, for instance, between trade-unions in the totalitarian states and in the democracies? In the totalitarian state a trade-union is an instrument used by the government to enforce duties, not to assert rights. Propaganda material which the government desires the workers to have is furnished to the trade-unions to be circulated to their members.

Our trade-unions, on the other hand, are solely the instruments of the workers themselves. They represent the workers in their relations with the government and with management and they are free to develop their own opinions without government help or interference. The concepts of our trade-unions and those in totalitarian countries are drastically different. There is little mutual understanding.

I think the best example one can give of this basic difference of the use of terms is "the right to work". The Soviet Union insists that this is a basic right which it alone can guarantee because it alone provides full employment by the government. But the right to work in the Soviet Union means the assignment of workers to do whatever task is given to them by the government without an opportunity for the people to participate in the decision that the government should do this. A society in which everyone works is not necessarily a free society and may indeed be a slave society; on the other hand, a society in which there is widespread economic insecurity can turn freedom into a barren and vapid right for millions of people. We in the United States have come to realize it means freedom to choose one's job, to work or not to work as one desires. We, in the United States, have come to realize, however, that people have a right to demand that their government will not allow them to starve because as individuals that cannot find work of the kind they are accustomed to doing and this is a decision brought about by public opinion which came as a result of the great depression in which many people were out of work, but we would not consider in the United States that we have gained any freedom if we were compelled to follow a dictatorial assignment to work where and when we were told. The right of choice would seem to us an important, fundamental freedom.

I have great sympathy with the Russian people. They love their country and have always defended it valiantly against invaders. They have been through a period of revolution, as a result of which they were for a time cut off from outside contact. They have not lost their resulting suspicion of other countries and the great difficulty is today that their government encourages this suspicion and seems to believe that force alone will bring them respect.

We, in the democracies, believe in a kind of international respect and action which is reciprocal. We do not think others should treat us differently from the way they wish to be treated. It is interference in other countries that especially stirs up antagonism against the Soviet Government. If it wishes to feel secure in developing its economic and political theories within it territory, then it should grant others that same security. We believe in the freedom of people to make their own mistakes. We do not interfere with them and they should not interfere with others.

The basic problem confronting the world today, as I said in the beginning, is the preservation of human freedom for the individual and consequently for the society of which he his a part. We are fighting this battle again today as it was fought at the time of the French Revolution and at the time of the American Revolution. The issue of human liberty is as decisive now as it was then. I want to give you my conception of what is meant in my country by freedom of the individual.

Long ago in London during a discussion with Mr. Vyshinsky, he told me there was no such thing as freedom for the individual in the world. All freedom of the individual was conditioned by the rights of other individuals. That, of course, I granted. I said: "We approach the question from a different point of view; we here in the United Nations are trying to develop ideals which will be broader in outlook, which will consider first the rights of man, which will consider what makes man more free: not governments, but man."

The totalitarian state typically places the will of the people second to decrees promulgated by a few men at the top.

Naturally there must always be consideration of the rights of others; but in a democracy this is not a restriction. Indeed, in our democracies we make our freedoms secure because each of us is expected to respect the rights of others and we are free to make our own laws.

Freedom for our peoples is not only a right, but also a tool. Freedom of speech, freedom of the press, freedom of information, freedom of assembly—these are not just abstract ideals to us; they are tools with which we create a way of life, a way of life in which we can enjoy freedom.

Sometimes the processes of democracy are slow, and I have known some of our leaders to say that a benevolent dictatorship would accomplish the ends desired in a much shorter time than it takes to go through the democratic processes of discussion and the slow formation of public opinion. But there is no way of insuring that a dictatorship will remain benevolent or that power once in the hands of a few will be returned to the people without struggle or revolution. This we have learned by experience and we accept the slow processes of democracy because we know that short-cuts compromise principles on which no compromise is possible.

The final expression of the opinion of the people with us is through free and honest elections, with valid choices on basic issues and candidates. The secret ballot is an essential to free elections but you must have a choice before you. I have heard my husband say many times that a people need never lose their freedom if they kept their right to a secret ballot and if they used that secret ballot to the full.

Basic decisions of our society are made through the expressed will of the people. That is why when we see these liberties threatened, instead of falling apart, our nation becomes unified and our democracies come together as a unified group in spite of our varied backgrounds and many racial strains.

In the Unites States we have a capitalistic economy. That is because public opinion favors that type of economy under the conditions in which we live. But we have imposed certain restraints; for instance, we have anti-trust laws. These are the legal evidence of the determination of the American people to maintain an economy of free competition and not to allow monopolies to take away the people's freedom.

Our trade-unions grows stronger because the people come to believe that this is the proper way to guarantee the rights of the workers and that the right to organize and to bargain collectively keeps the balance between the actual producer and the investor of money and the manager in industry who watches over the man who works with his hands and who produces the materials which are our tangible wealth.

In the United States we are old enough not to claim perfection. We recognize that we have some problems of discrimination but we find steady progress being made in the solution of these problems. Through normal democratic processes we are coming to understand our needs and how we can attain full equality for all our people. Free discussion on the subject is permitted. Our Supreme Court has recently rendered decisions to clarify a number of our laws to guarantee the rights of all.

The U.S.S.R. claims it has reached a point where all races within her borders are officially considered equal and have equal rights and they insist they have no discrimination where minorities are concerned.

This is a laudable objective but there are other aspects of the development of freedom for the individual which are essential before the mere absence of discrimination is worth much, and these are lacking in the Soviet Union. Unless they are being denied freedoms which they want and which they see other people have, people do not usually complain of discrimination. It is these other freedoms—the basic freedoms of speech, of the press, of religion and conscience, of assembly, of fair trial and freedom from arbitrary arrest and punishment, which a totalitarian government cannot safely give its people and which give meaning to freedom from discrimination.

It is my belief, and I am sure it is also yours, that the struggle for democracy and freedom is a critical struggle, for their preservation is essential to the great objective of the United Nations to maintain international peace and security.

Among free men the end cannot justify the means. We know the patterns of totalitarianism—the single political party, the control of schools, press, radio, the arts, the sciences, and the church to support autocratic authority; these are the age-old patterns against which men have struggled for three thousand years. These are the signs of reaction, retreat, and retrogression.

The United Nations must hold fast to the heritage of freedom won by the struggle of its peoples; it must help us to pass it on to generations to come.

The development of the ideal of freedom and its translation into the everyday life of the people in great areas of the earth is the product of the efforts of many peoples. It is the fruit of a long tradition of vigorous thinking and courageous action. No one race and no one people can claim to have done all the work to achieve greater dignity for human beings and greater freedom to develop human personality. In each generation and in each country there must be a continuation of the struggle and new steps forward must be taken since this is preeminently a field in which to stand still is to retreat.

The field of human rights in not one in which compromise on fundamental principles are possible. The work of the Commission on Human Rights is illustrative. The Declaration of Human Rights provides: " Everyone has the right to leave any country, including his own." The Soviet Representative said he would agree to this right if a single phrase was added to it—"in accordance with the procedure laid down in the laws of that country." It is obvious that to accept this would be not only to compromise but to nullify the right stated. This case forcefully illustrates the importance of the proposition that we must ever be alert not to compromise fundamental human rights merely for the sake of reaching unanimity and thus lose them.

As I see it, it is not going to be easy to attain unanimity with respect to our different concepts of government and human rights. The struggle is bound to be difficult and one in which we must be firm but patient. If we adhere faithfully to our principles I think it is possible for us to maintain freedom and to do so peacefully and without recourse to force.

The future must see the broadening of human rights throughout the world. People who have glimpsed freedom will never be content until they have secured it for themselves. In a true sense, human rights are a fundamental object of law and government in a just society. Human rights exist to the degree that they are respected by people in relations with each other and by governments in relations with their citizens.

The world at large is aware of the tragic consequences for human beings ruled by totalitarian systems. If we examine Hitler's rise to power, we see how the chains are forged which keep the individual a slave and we can see many similarities in the way things are accomplished in other countries. Politically men must be free to discuss and to arrive at as many facts as possible and there must be at least a two-party system in a country because when there is only one political party, too many things can be subordinated to the interests of that one party and it becomes a tyrant and not an instrument of democratic government.

The propaganda we have witnessed in the recent past, like that we perceive in these days, seeks to impugn, to undermine, and to destroy the liberty and independence of peoples. Such propaganda poses to all peoples the issue whether to doubt their heritage of rights and therefore to compromise the principles by which they live, or try to accept the challenge, redouble their vigilance, and stand steadfast in the struggle to maintain and enlarge human freedoms.

People who continue to be denied the respect to which they are entitled as human beings will not acquiesce forever in such denial.

The Charter of the United Nations is a guiding beacon along the way to the achievement of human rights and fundamental freedoms throughout the world. The immediate test is not only the extent to which human rights and freedoms have already been achieved, but the direction in which the world is moving. Is there a faithful compliance with the objectives of the Charter if some countries continue to curtail human rights and freedoms instead of to promote the universal respect for an observance of human rights and freedoms for all as called for by the Charter?

The place to discuss the issue of human rights is in the forum of the United Nations. The United Nations has been set up as the common meeting ground for nations, where we can consider together our mutual problems and take advantage of our differences in experience. It is inherent in our firm attachment to democracy and freedom that we stand always ready to use the fundamental democratic procedures of honest discussion and negotiation. It is now as always our hope that despite the wide differences in approach we face in the world today, we can with mutual good faith in the principles of the United Nations Charter, arrive at a common basis of understanding. We are here to join the meetings of this great international Assembly which meets in your beautiful capital city of Paris. Freedom for the individual is an inseparable part of the cherished traditions of France. As one of the Delegates from the United States I pray Almighty God that we may win another victory here for the rights and freedoms of all men.

§ TO THE WOMEN OF THE WORLD *

This first Assembly of the United Nations marks the second attempt of the peoples of the world to live peacefully in a democratic world community. This new chance for peace was won through the joint efforts of men and women working for common ideals of human freedom at a time when the need for united effort broke down barriers of race, creed and sex.

In view of the variety of tasks which women performed so notably and valiantly during the war, we are gratified that seventeen women representatives and advisers, representatives of eleven Member States, are taking part at the beginning of this new phase of international effort. We hope their participation in the work of the United

---

* Text of an open letter to the women of the world from the women delegates and advisers at the first Assembly of the United Nations. The open letter, dated February 12, 1946, was signed by: Mrs. Eleanor Roosevelt, Mrs. M. Lefaucheaux (France), Miss Minerva Bernardino (The Dominican Republic), Mrs. Dalen (Norway), Mrs. Verwey (The Netherlands), and 12 other women delegates to the General Assembly.

Nations Organization may grow and increase insight and in skill. To this end we call on the Governments of the world to encourage women everywhere to take a more active part in national and international affairs, and on women who are conscious of their opportunities to come forward and share in the work of peace and reconstruction as they did in war and resistance.

We recognize that women in various parts of the world are at different stages of participation in the life of their community, that some of them are prevented by law from assuming full rights of citizenship, and that they therefore may see their immediate problems somewhat differently.

Finding ourselves in agreement on these points, we wish as a group to advise the women of all our countries of our strong belief that an important opportunity and responsibility confront the women of the United Nations:

- first, to recognize the progress women have made during the war and to participate actively in the effort to improve the standards of life in their own countries and in the pressing work of reconstruction, so that there will be qualified women ready to accept responsibility when new opportunities arise;

- second, to train their children, boys and girls alike, to understand world problems and the need for international cooperation, as well as the problems of their own countries;

- third, not to permit themselves to be misled by anti-democratic movements now or in the future;

- fourth, to recognize that the goal of full participation in the life and responsibilities of their countries and of the world community is a common objective toward which the women of the world should assist one another."

§ SHE SAW CLEARLY; SHE SPOKE SIMPLY

By Adlai Ewing Steveson [*]

I come here for the second time in little more than a year, sad in heart and in spirit. The United States, the United Nations -- the world -- has lost one of its great citizens. Mrs. Eleanor Roosevelt is dead and a cherished friend of all mankind is gone.

Yesterday I said I lost more than a friend; I had lost an inspiration. For, she would rather light candles than curse the darkness and her glow had warmed the world.

My country mourns her and I know that all in this assembly mourn with us. But even as we do, the sadness that we

[*] Eulogy for Eleanor Roosevelt delivered at the United Nations on November 9, 1962. Ambassador Stevenson was U.S. Permanent Representative to the United Nations during the Kennedy and Johnson Administrations, from 1961 to 1965.

share is enlivened by the faith in her fellow man and his future, which filled the heart of this strong and gentle woman.

She imparted this faith not only to those who shared the privilege of knowing her and of working by her side but to countless men, women, and children in every part of the world who loved her even as she loved them. For she embodied the vision and the will to achieve a world in which all men can walk in peace and dignity. And to this goal of a better life she dedicated her tireless energy and the strange strength of her extraordinary personality.

I don't think it amiss, Mr. President, to suggest that the United Nations is in no small way a memorial to her and to her aspirations. To it she gave the last 15 years of her restless spirit. She breathed life into this Organization. The United Nations has meaning and hope for millions, thanks to her labors, her love, no less than to her ideals; ideals that made her, only weeks after Franklyn Roosevelt's death, put aside all thoughts of peace and quiet after the tumult of their lives, to serve as one of this Nation's delegates to the first regular session of the General Assembly. Her duty then -- as always -- was to the living, to the world, to peace.

Some of you in this hall were present at that first historic assembly in London 17 years ago. More of you were witnesses to her work in subsequent assemblies in the years that followed. The members of the Third Committee -- the Committee in Social, humanitarian, and Cultural Questions

-- and the Commission on Human Rights, which she served so long as Chairman – you, in particular, will remember the warmth, the intelligence, and infectious buoyancy which she brought to her tasks. You know better than any of us the unceasing crusade that helped to give the world, after years of painstaking and patient travail, one of the noblest documents of mankind: the Universal Declaration of Human Rights.

This is not the time to recount the infinite services of this glorious and gracious lady; the list is as inexhaustible as her energies. But devotion to the world of the Charter, to the principles of the United Nations, to a world without war, to the brotherhood of man, underscored them all. And, happily for us all, she could communicate her devotion, her enthusiasm, to others. She saw clearly; she spoke simply. The power of her words came from the depth of her conviction.

'We must be willing,' she said, 'to learn the lesson that cooperation may imply compromise, but if it brings a world advance it is a gain for each individual nation. There will be those who doubt their ability to rise to these new heights, but the alternative is not possible to contemplate. We must build faith in the hearts of those who doubt, we must rekindle faith in ourselves when it grows dim, and find some kind of divine courage within us to keep on till on earth we have peace and good will among men.'

Albert Schweitzer wrote:

No ray of sunlight is ever lost, but the green which it wakes needs time to sprout, and it is not always granted to the sower to live to see the harvest. All work that is worth anything is done in faith.

While she lived, Mrs. Roosevelt rekindled that faith in ourselves. Now that she is gone, the legacy of her lifetime will do no less.

Mr. President, I trust you and the members of the Assembly will forgive me for having taken your time with these very personal thoughts. The issues we debate in this hall are many and grave. But I do not think that we are divided in our grief at the passing of this great and gallant human being -- who was called the First lady of the World.

HELVI SIPILÄ

Matthew Couper
Helvi Sipilä
2011
Pencil on paper
7" x 5" / 175mm x 135mm
www.mattcouper.com

Assistant - Undersecretary General of the U.N.

Helvi Sipilä
1915 ~ 2009
Finnish Diplomat.

Jonathan Cooper 2011

"Without our 'international lady' Helvi Sipilä, UNIFEM and work for women would not be what they are today. As a Deputy Secretary-General, she put women's affairs onto the UN agenda. Through her own example she has encouraged us women to work for a better future."

— Eeva Ahtisaari
Former First Lady of Finland

§ FINLAND'S INTERNATIONAL LADY

By Johanna Forsström and Anneli Mäkelä-Alitalo *

When she was chosen as the first female assistant secretary-general of the United Nations, Helvi Sipilä had a long background as a lawyer and organisational leader. At the UN her areas of responsibility were women's issues, social development and crime prevention. Sipilä also became the first woman to stand for the office of President of Finland.

Helvi Sipilä is the sort of person who understands changing times and the new attitudes and fresh challenges that they bring with them. When she announced the opening of her law firm on the front page of a daily newspaper in

---

* Originally published in "100 Faces from Finland. A Biographical Kaleidoscope," by the Finnish Literature Society (Suomalaisen Kirjallisuuden Seura, SKS) in 2000. Courtesy of SKS.

November 1943, she became the second woman in Finnish history to begin practising as a lawyer. Her additional voluntary work in the field of national and international co-operation led to ever more demanding duties, and in 1972 she was offered the position of an assistant secretary-general of the United Nations. Sipilä was the first woman to hold this important post, and she did so for almost ten years. After this she stood for the Finnish presidency in 1981 - another first for a woman. In short, it may be said that in her career Helvi Sipilä followed many new and challenging paths in the field of the enhancement and defence of women's rights.

Helvi Maukola was born in Helsinki in 1915, the daughter of Vilho Maukola, a wealthy farm owner, and Aleksandra Lucinda Manner. She grew up to be an independent and firm-minded woman who did not, however, lack the ability to take other people's feelings into consideration. If we bear a few facts in mind, we may better understand the decisiveness and strength shown by the young Helvi Maukola (Helvi Sipilä from 1939 onwards) as a pioneering female Law graduate. When she was awarded her Higher Law (Bachelor of Laws) certificate on 15 March 1939, she became Finland's thirty-eighth law graduate and, upon taking the oath two days later at the Turku Appeal Court, the eighteenth woman in Finland to begin practical training at an appeal court. Since this training occurred under exceptional conditions, she was awarded the title of Deputy Judge (Master of Laws) by the Appeal Court on 19 December 1941, being the sixteenth woman in Finland to gain this qualification. It was difficult for women to make a career in the law at a time when women Law graduates were a rarity and women judges were often regarded almost with suspicion. But Helvi Sipilä pushed ahead purposefully along the path that she had chosen.

Sipilä's period of court practice began in Hollola, the judicial district in which her home at Kärkölä was situated. It was marked by exceptional circumstances for the nation: on 3 September the Second World War broke out, and on 30 November the Winter War began for Finland. The peace concluded with the Soviet Union in March 1940 was a brief one, and Finland was driven into the Continuation War in June 1941. Sipilä and other female jurists constituted a significant labour reserve at the courts when men were forced to leave their civilian jobs. Sipilä was then working in a supernumerary capacity as a court clerk of the Hollola judicial district, and in these special circumstances, one action of the Turku Appeal Court was to assign her to sit as a judge at sessions lasting more than three weeks held in Helsinki Parish, which was then part of the Helsinki judicial district, and at the district courts of other municipalities in October 1941. This work was sufficient for Sipilä to be granted the title of Deputy Judge. Her 'war service' continued in the form of supernumerary posts at the Administrative Court and the Supreme Court.

It had, however, long been Helvi Sipilä's real dream to work as an attorney, and in November 1943 she opened her own office. For Sipilä this event had great significance: she was now a real lawyer, and her application for membership of the Finnish Lawyers' Association (*Suomen asianajajaliitto)* was accepted on 31 May 1946. Sipilä became involved in a number of voluntary activities in addition to her regular job. Her voluntary work for various national and international bodies led to ever more demanding tasks. Between 1960 and 1972 she represented Finland in a number of UN organisations. When an offer by the UN secretary-general to appoint her an assistant secretary-general followed, she felt unable, for the sake of her own country and the world in general, to say no to this position. She was obliged to leave her law office in Helsinki and to move abroad, first to New York and later to Vienna, for a period of more than nine years. Her name was, however, retained in the name of the firm, even though she ceased to own it in August 1972.

Her work as a lawyer had accustomed Helvi Sipilä to defending those in weak positions, and she now expanded her defensive role to cover the world economy and needy people in developing countries. As an assistant secretary-general, she was in charge of the Center for Social Development and Humanitarian Affairs, which dealt, among other things, with women's issues and crime prevention. The major events during her period as an assistant secretary-general were the International Women's Year in 1975 and the first United Nations world conference for the advancement of women, of which she was the secretary-general.

A keen supporter of the scouting movement, Helvi Sipilä served as a member of the international committee of the World Association of Girl Guides and Girl Scouts and was also an adviser to new member states in the movement. In her actions she followed the motto: "Every scout is every scout's comrade". It was precisely the scouting spirit that made Sipilä into a leader who did not issue orders from above but walked the same path as her fellows and planned all her actions in collaboration with others and with consideration for the views of others. Sipilä realised that helping the individual also involves changing the world and that it was necessary to influence public opinion and national leaders in order to make the world wake up and take notice of the prevailing injustice, oppression and suffering.

It was in the scouting spirit that Helvi Sipilä served at the UN, where she made great contributions towards improving the status of women in particular. She refused to regard their inferior position as a problem in isolation, since women, children and men are bound together in the same society; but she nevertheless considered that women's rights were (and are) neglected in many societies. Since the subordinate position of women is a great obstacle to development, it is essential - for the sake of men and children as well - that women should be trusted and given the right to participate in decision-making, and that they should be granted general, recognised equality. Sipilä believes that change must start specifically with women.

Helvi Sipilä's work on behalf of women and men did not end with her term as a UN assistant secretary-general. She continued to play an active role as the chairwoman of the

UN Women's Development Fund's Finnish association; instead of dealing with global-level issues, she now devoted herself to helping individual human beings through development aid. After her return to Finland Sipilä also took another step in opening to women the path to the top of the political hierarchy: in the presidential election of 1982, then still conducted by means of an electoral college, the National Liberal Party chose her as the first woman candidate ever to stand.

§ POWER IS THUS ALSO A FORCE FOR GOOD

By Rachel Mayanja *

This is the first Helvi Sipila seminar since her death last May. It is thus also an occasion to celebrate her as a true champion and pioneer of women's rights. At the time of her passing, the United Nations Secretary-General praised Helvi Sipila as a women's rights advocate and the effectiveness of her leadership. Her legacy serves as a reminder that no effort should be spared to ensure the equal participation of women in decision-making in all areas of life. It is only fitting that this year's seminar focuses on "Women and Power", in memory of Helvi Sipilä.

In 1972, Helvi Sipilä became the first woman to be

* Opening remarks by Ms. Rachel Mayanja, UN Special Adviser for Gender Issues and Advancement of Women, to the Fifth International Helvi Sipilä Seminar (United Nations Headquarters, March 4, 2010).

appointed an Assistant Secretary-General of the United Nations, a remarkable achievement at a time when 97 per cent of United Nations senior management (D1 and above) was male. She headed the Centre for Social Development and Humanitarian Affairs, which included the UN Division for the Advancement of Women, until her retirement from the Organization in 1980. Ms. Sipilä used her leadership position in the United Nations to advocate effectively for women's rights.

During her tenure, Ms. Sipilä served as the Secretary-General for the first World Conference on Women, in Mexico City, in 1975. She pointedly noted that the Conference was the first intergovernmental meeting at which women formed part of virtually all delegations, and she expressed her hope that it would set a precedent for equal representation of women and men in all future international meetings, whether on political or economic affairs, on disarmament, trade or human settlement. Ms. Sipilä was also instrumental in the founding of the United Nations Development Fund for Women (UNIFEM), then known as the United Nations Voluntary Fund for the Advancement of Women.

This seminar series was started in March 2006, in honour of Helvi Sipilä's work and her contribution to the Commission on the Status of Women, as well as to other international and national women's organizations. The seminars recognize Helvi Sipilä's effective use of her leadership position, and power, in the United Nations to push for gender equality and empowerment of women. She systematically reminded her predominantly male leadership of the need to fully utilize all the human resources of the world, women as well as men.

Helvi Sipilä demonstrated the effectiveness of women's leadership throughout her long life. She was an impressive role model, and her memory will serve as a reminder to all of us that we must finish the job of realizing the equal access of women and men to leadership positions everywhere, including at the United Nations.

We can rightfully be proud of the progress made in the promotion of gender equality and the empowerment of women since that first World Conference on Women in 1975. 2010 marks the 15th anniversary of the adoption of the Beijing Declaration and Platform for Action, at the Fourth World Conference on Women in 1995. At this session, the Commission on the Status of Women will undertake a review of the implementation of the Platform and of the outcomes of the twenty-third special session of the General Assembly held in 2000. It will also contribute to shaping a gender perspective towards the full realization of the Millennium Development Goals. The session will focus on an exchange of experiences, good practices and lessons learned with a view to overcoming remaining obstacles and challenges.

There have been noticeable gains for women and girls. Globally in 2007, women accounted for 39 per cent of all people engaged in paid employment outside of agriculture, a small but important increase from 35 per cent in 1990. In 2008, women's labour force participation reached an estimated 52.6 per cent. Access to education has increased for girls at all levels, particularly in primary education. In 2007, there were 96 girls for each 100 boys enrolled in first grade, compared with 92 girls in 1999. In some countries, women now outnumber men at tertiary level. The Convention on the Elimination of All Forms of Discrimination against Women has reached almost universal ratification, with 186 States being party to the treaty. Work on the Convention was one of the significant efforts of the Commission on the Status of Women during the period that Helvi Sipila headed the Commission's Secretariat in the 1970s.

Policies to address HIV/AIDS increasingly place specific emphasis on prevention, treatment and care for women. A growing number of States have in place comprehensive legal, policy, and institutional frameworks to end violence against women and girls, and support services are increasingly available to victims/survivors. In December 2009, women held 18.9 per cent of seats in single/lower chambers of parliament, compared to 11.3 per cent in 1995. 25 countries had reached the 30 per cent threshold of more women parliamentarians, a significant increase from only five countries in 1995.

In many countries, national mechanisms for gender equality, including ministries and offices in the Executive Branch, as well as Parliamentary committees and independent, advisory and monitoring bodies play a key role in the promotion of gender equality. The gender mainstreaming strategy is increasingly applied across all sectors, supported by a wider range of tools, capacity-building programmes and training. Monitoring and evaluation of efforts has improved.

Despite these advances, the Beijing Platform for Action has yet to be fully implemented. Progress in improving women's lives, eliminating discrimination and achieving equality has been uneven across countries and regions. We have also been moving too slowly to meet the Millennium Development Goals (MDGs), and there has been almost no progress with regard to MDG 5, to improve maternal health. Every year, 536,000 women and girls die as a result of pregnancy or childbirth. Women are more likely than men to be living in poverty.

Illiteracy remains a serious constraint for women, who continue to account for nearly two thirds of the 776 million illiterate adults in the world. Gender wage-gaps persist in all parts of the world. The global economic and financial crisis has created new hurdles to women's employment, and estimates suggest that unemployment rates are higher for women than men. More women than men remain trapped in insecure and often unpaid work. The deliberate targeting of civilians and the use of sexual violence against women continues on a large scale in ongoing conflicts.

Discrimination in law has not been eliminated, and discriminatory application and enforcement of laws prevents women from enjoying equal rights and access to resources and opportunities. Negative gender stereotypes based on societal beliefs and attitudes constrain their opportunities and choices. Women continue to be responsible for most domestic and caregiving work. This unequal sharing of responsibilities negatively impacts their educational and employment opportunities, and limits their involvement in public life.

Your seminar will focus on the question of women and power. Power is defined as the ability or capacity to perform or act effectively. It also gives a number of synonyms for power, including might and authority. Some of the well-known quotations on power make us not to want, or encounter it ("Power tends to corrupt and absolute power corrupts absolutely"). Yet John Stuart Mill, in his essay "On liberty" advised that "The only purpose for which power can be rightfully exercised over any member of a civilized community, against his will, is to prevent harm to others. His own good, either physical or moral, is not a sufficient warrant". Power can be wielded in many different ways, and we are faced with power constantly in our daily lives. Power – especially in the meaning of authority – is critical for progress and advancement.

Helvi Sipilä surely wielded power. She used it to advocate for the improvement of the status of women in all parts of the world. She saw the harm that was done to women – and societies – by discrimination, violence and abuse. She understood that lack of power – in the home, in the family, in the community – kept women in positions of inferiority and subjected to exploitation. She saw that unequal power relations between women and men perpetuated stereotypes that harmed women and held societies back, everywhere.

Power is thus also a force for good. It is necessary to overcome the obstacles and challenges that continue to be barriers for women's enjoyment of their rights, their access to justice and equal opportunities. Power is necessary to protect women from harm and violence.

The commemoration of the 15-year anniversary of the adoption of the Beijing Declaration and Platform for Action is an opportune time to consider the role of power in the promotion of gender equality and women's enjoyment of their human rights.The focus of this article will be on the changing
roles   of

§ CHANGING ROLES OF WOMEN IN THE DEVELOPING REGIONS OF THE WORLD

By Helvi Sipilä *

The focus of this article will be on the changing roles of women in the developing regions, though I do not wish to suggest that those roles have not been changing in other parts of the world, as well. In industrialized countries women's role in gainful occupations outside their homes has been changing more rapidly and more fully than in countries where industrialization is still less advanced. These countries have also provided education for everyone, making it possible for large numbers of women to achieve academic training in a variety of fields, including those previously dominated by males. In countries where the basic needs of the majority of the

_____

* Originally published in the Journal of International Affairs 30:2 (1976-77), 183-90. Courtesy of the Journal of International Affairs.

people are being met, most women also benefit from health and other social services, from adequate nutrition, and satisfactory housing. Some women are, of course, enjoying the same rights in the developing regions, and there are without doubt women in developed regions who lack such rights, but in both cases these women are in the minority.

These are also reasons for not lumping all developing countries together under one heading. There are enormous differences from country to country due to different cultural, religious, political, ideological and economic backgrounds.

One question which is often raised, particularly in connection with United Nations activities for the advancement of women, is the advisability of changing the traditional situation of women. In other words, how can the integration of women in the development effort take place without changing important cultural values?

Although reservations in this regard are, to a certain extent, justified, we must differentiate between values which should be respected and retained and situations of underdevelopment which need to be changed. The integration of women in the development process was first included as one of the important goals of the International Development Strategy for the Second United Nations Development Decade – adopted by the Twenty-Fifth United Nations General Assembly. It was also one of the three major objectives – equality, development and peace – of the International Women's Year 1975. The same objectives were adopted for the Decade for Women (1976-1985), proclaimed by the Thirtieth Session of the General Assembly in December 1975.

The three objectives are obviously interrelated. The full integration of women in the life of society in all fields and at all levels as equal partners with men cannot be achieved unless women have equal rights and obligations with men. The third objective, namely women's increasing contribution to the development of friendly relations among States and the strengthening of world peace, is but one aspect of women's full involvement in the life of society.

A large number of recommendations for the improvement of the situation of women are contained in the World Plan of Action adopted by the representatives of the one hundred and thirty-three governments who participated in the International Women's Year World Conference in Mexico City in June-July 1975. These recommendations as well as those contained in the Declaration of Mexico, in the two Regional Plans of Action and in thirty-four resolutions, were subsequently endorsed by the United Nations General Assembly. The Assembly as well as the Economic and Social Council have also adopted a number of additional resolutions, which should be implemented during the Decade for Women. If these efforts prove fruitful, the situation and role of women will change drastically. This applies to the developing as well as the developed countries, although the needs as well as the means will vary from country to country.

The World Plan of Action is the first comprehensive socio-economic program for the international community as a whole. It suggests a large number of practical measures to be taken toward achieving the goals of the Year and the Decade. While it calls for action at national, regional, and global levels, national action will be the most critical because of the differing needs of every country and the rights of sovereign states to determine what measures they will adopt.

A number of objectives are expected to be achieved within the first five-year period (1976-1980). The governments are expected to adopt short, medium, and long term targets and objectives toward implementing the Plan. One of the important pre-conditions or implementation is the establishment of an inter-disciplinary and multi-sectoral machinery within governments for accelerating the achievement of equal opportunities for women and their full integration in national life.

Of course no area in which national action is needed to improve the situation of women should be viewed in isolation. All are closely interrelated and measures to effect change should be an integral part of broader national development strategies and programmes.

The first area where improvement is necessary is that of international co-operation and the strengthening of international peace, which requires, *inter alia*, that women have equal opportunities with men to represent their country in all international for a where issues related to international co-operation and peace are discussed. Included here would be all meetings of the organizations of the United Nations system, including those of the Security Council and all conferences on disarmament and international peace.

The World Plan of Action recognizes that even though women make up 50% of the population of the world, only a minute percentage of them are involved in national decision-making. Therefore, their needs and their views are often overlooked in planning for development. They are usually unaware of the implications of development plans and programmes and less inclined to support their implementation. Many women also lack the education and the training, civic awareness and self-confidence to participate actively in political life.

Special efforts are, therefore, needed to increase women's participation in public and political life at every level. Women who, until recent decades, did not have political rights anywhere in the world, must become aware of their responsibilities as citizens and of the problems affecting society. This requires policy decisions, special emphasis on the recruitment and promotion of women to positions of leadership, and public information activities.

Another area where action is needed involves education and training, key factors in social progress and the reduction of the socio-economic gaps between men and women. We know, for example, that female illiteracy is far higher than male-illiteracy. We also know that the lack of education or training in basic skills is a key element in the vicious cycle of under-development, low productivity and poor conditions of health. This becomes all the more serious because women are mainly responsible for the training of the children during their formative years. If target dates for the eradication of illiteracy were set and high priority was given to programmes for women and girls between the ages of 16 and 25, great changes could take place in the long term development of human resources. Many other suggestions are made in the Plan for improved educational opportunities for women.

CARLO URBANI

Matthew Couper
Carlo Urbani
2011
Pencil on paper
7" x 5" / 175mm x 135mm
www.mattcouper.com

Carlo Urbani

1956 ~ 2003
Italian physician who
identified SARS

Matthew Cooper 2011

"Shortly before Dr. Urbani became ill, his wife worried about the danger in which he was putting himself. Dr. Urbani replied: 'If I cannot work in such situations, what am I here for - answering emails and pushing paper?' Carlo Urbani has given us WHO its best - not pushing paper, but pushing back the assault of poverty and disease."

— Lee Jong-wook
Former Director-General
of the World Health Organization

§ IT WAS A TRICKY CALL

By Andreas S. von Warburg

Between November 2002 and July 2003, a pandemic killed more than 900 people worldwide. Cause of death? - SARS, an acronym for the Severe Acute Respiratory Syndrome. The virus spread in a matter of weeks from a small hospital in the Honk Hong province of China to rapidly infect individuals in some 37 countries around the world. By 2004, when the virus was fully contained, almost 5,000 had been infected, with fatality rates reaching over 10%.

The first to identify the virus was Dr. Carlo Urbani, an Italian epidemiologist and infectious disease expert. In 2003 Carlo, while working for the World Health Organization (WHO) as Director of infectious diseases for the Western Pacific Region, was called into the French Hospital in Hanoi to visit a patient with uncharacteristic influenza symptoms. He soon realized that the patient, American businessman Johnny Chen, did not have the flu, but a new and highly contagious disease.

Before Chen's case, according to a 2003 New York Times report, rumors of a mysterious pneumonia had been coming out of the Guangdong region of southern China, but the Chinese authorities had been close-lipped, even instructing local reporters to ignore it. Although no one then realized the significance of those rumors, Chen had stayed in the same Hong Kong hotel where a 64-year-old Guangdong doctor was staying while in town for a wedding. Investigators, according to the same report, theorize that the doctor infected 12 other guests, several from the same floor, who carried the disease to Singapore, Toronto and elsewhere.

"It was a tricky call," later reported the New York Times. "There is nothing as telltale about the disease as the bleeding of a hemorrhagic fever or the bumps of a pox, and its symptoms mimic other respiratory conditions."

Once he identified the dangerous and highly contagious nature of the virus, Carlo immediately notified the WHO, triggering the most effective response to a major epidemic in history, which included the Vietnamese Health Ministry's isolation of patients and screening of travelers, thus slowing the early pace of the epidemic.

"That took a lot of guts," said Dr. Kevin L. Palmer, WHO's regional specialist in parasitic diseases and a friend of

Urbani's. "He's a foreigner telling the Vietnamese government that it looks very bad. But he had a lot of credibility with the government people, and he was a pretty gregarious kind of character."

His early warning touched off a massive response that helped save the lives of millions of people around the world, but not his own. On March 29, 2003, Carlo succumbed to the SARS virus and died in a Thai hospital in Bangkok, where he had flown into from Hanoi a few weeks earlier to participate in a conference on the subject of childhood parasites. He was 46. Carlo, who after identifying the virus worked tirelessly side by side with his patients in order to contain the epidemic and save as many lives as possible, didn't realized until the very end that he himself had been infected. He started feeling feverish on the plane, and soon after was transported to the hospital where he died. He was one of the first to be killed by the virus - one of 80 people, including many healthcare workers - who, according to the World Health Organization, were infected by Chen.

"Life urged him to leave behind the comforts of Italy so he could be closer to the poor of developing countries," said Jordan Ryan, then United Nations Resident Coordinator in Vietnam, remembering his friend and colleague during a memorial in 2004. "And life made him rush from his WHO office to that Hanoi hospital to care for those falling gravely ill to SARS, before any of us knew what SARS was."

"Yes, Carlo's life is a lesson for us all," Ryan said. "It demonstrates how best to respond today to the crises and problems, promises and opportunities we face. Carlo has left behind with us his path of triumphs. And now it is the time for each of us to create our own."

Carlo's experience and dedication have indeed touched many, both within his circle of friends and colleagues, and within the international medical community.

"When people became very concerned in the hospital, he was there every day, collecting samples, talking to the staff and strengthening infection control procedures," Pascale Brudon, WHO Representative in Vietnam, said in a statement after his death. It was dangerous work, but Carlo told his wife Giuliani, "If I can't work in such situations, what am I here for? Answering e-mails, going to cocktail parties and pushing paper?"

According to a biography published by the Lancelet, [*] Carlo first worked for the World Health Organization, a specialized agency of the United Nations, in 1993, when a colleague, doctor Lorenzo Savioli, asked him to research hookworms in the Maldives. He had left his job as head of the infectious disease department of the Macerata Hospital, in the Marche region of Italy, and accepted the post, friends said, because he wanted to be back in the third world and working with patients.

---

[*] The Lancet, Volume 361, Issue 9367, Page 1481, 26 April 2003.

"Nobody at headquarters was going to believe we were spending our days in the Maldives over fecal samples," Savioli told the New York Times in an interview after Carlo's death.

Carlo was not new to identifying the spread of contagious and infectious diseases in developing countries. His work in the Maldives led him to study and treat hookworms around the world, and to be the first to report transmission of schistosoma mansoni in Mauritania. His interest in the subject was both medical and philosophical. Carlo thought his work could save lives. While working for WHO, he decided to take postgraduate courses in malaria and medical parasitology at the Istituto Superiore di Sanita (the leading technical and scientific public body of the Italian National Health Service) in Rome, Italy. Following his studies he moved on to Médecins Sans Frontières (MSF, or Doctors Without Borders) in 1995, working in Cambodia to effectively control schistosoma mekongi.

After joining MSF, Carlo kept worked in various parts of Asia – mostly Vietnam and the Philipines – for WHO as a consultant in parasitology. Well into his medical activity in the developing world, in April 1999 Carlo became president of the Italian branch of MSF, pushing the branch into working with the poorest of the poor, with Gypsies in Rome and with African and Albanian boat people who were landing on the coasts of Sicily and Calabria. The same year, the organization founded by Bernard Kouchner won the Nobel Prize for Peace, and in

December 1999 Carlo travelled to Oslo as a member of the official MSF delegation to accept the prize.

"He is remembered as a highly motivated doctor who insisted on remaining an active participant with vulnerable people around the world," MSF said in a statement after Carlo's death. "MSF remembers his positive attitude and uncompromising support along with his exceptionally generous nature."

§ A DROP OF WATER IN THE DESERT

By Andreas S. von Warburg [*]

- How would you describe your husband Carlo to those who have never heard about his story and the stories of the many international civil servants who died in the line of duty?

- Carlo was a man who loved life, his family, and the weakest people of our society. I believe he had always had deep inside his heart a burning desire to be a doctor and use medicine to address important issues; and his later specialization in highly contagious and tropical diseases gave him the tools to help remove those barriers he had always wanted to remove.

---

[*] Interview to Giuliana Chiorrini, wife of the late Dr. Carlo Urbani.

– Carlo dedicated his entire life to helping others. Were his love for medicine, his courage of conviction, and his desire to practice in the most remote regions of the world always evident? How did they originate?

– As a young man, the pleasure in committing himself to helping others was evident in his interest for the welfare of the country and its people, in his faith and involvement with the local parish, in his efforts to assist the less privileged, in his search for human solidarity, especially towards the weakest, those who suffer and the victims of discrimination and intolerance.

I still remember Carlo's passion in organizing holiday trips for handicapped people, in finding medicine supplies to help the work of missionaries in Africa. He was the embodiment of a "médecin sans frontiers," a real doctor without borders.

It is hard to say when his interest for the Third World manifested itself. It is indeed a mix of diverse factors that nurtured his passion: professional experiences with non-governmental organizations – Mani Tese and UNITALSI in particular –, books, and further readings. But also, the many extraordinary people he met throughout his life: individuals who showed their love for mankind and peace.

– How would you describe Carlo's experience with Médecins Sans Frontières (Doctors Without Borders)?

– In Italy, Carlo worked initially as a primary care physician and later as a surgeon at a Hospital in Macerata. He left his position in Italy to address the needs of the thousands of people in need and to be the spokesperson for those whose lives have been stripped of all dignities and health.

– *And the Nobel Peace Prize?*

– As President of Doctors Without Borders in Italy, he was included in the official delegation who traveled to Oslo, Norway, in December 1999 to receive the Nobel Peace Prize. "This prize is not for us, but for the idea that health and dignity are inseparable in the human being," he said on that occasion.

– *His job at the World Health Organization, one of the many entities of the United Nations system, put Carlo in contact with – almost by definition – a much more bureaucratic reality compared to Doctors Without Borders. And the approach to medicine as well is much different. Any regret? Any disappointment?*

– To work for the World Health Organization was Carlo's dream. In 2000, he finally joined the organization as a Coordinator for Health Policies in South East Asia. It was a radical choice that changed the future of his entire family: from that point on my children and I became world citizens.

Carlo was extremely satisfied with what he was accomplishing at the WHO, always in his conviction that even one drop of water in the desert is a step forward.

He lived his job with total devotion and he never denounced any delusion or disappointment, even when he was put face-to-face with the most onerous commitments.

– In those years, have you ever thought about returning to a more "tranquil" life in Italy and leave the Third World and its needs behind?

– As his family, we had never thought to go back to Italy. We all fully shared his life of work, of discovering new horizons, of goals already achieved and goals still to be reached.

– Carlo was the first to identify the Severe Acute Respiratory Syndrome, or SARS, the fast-spreading form of viral pneumonia originating in Vietnam that cannot be treated with antibiotics. Even when the situation was becoming dangerous, he was at the hospital every day, collecting samples and tracing the paths of infection. Eventually he contracted the disease himself. What was his biggest fear?

– He was the one who first discovered SARS and how it was dangerously spreading; but he was not worried about himself; he was worried about the others. He feared that an increasing portion of the world population was in great danger. He fought the spreading of the virus until the end and his attempt was successful.

– *Carlo's work in Vietnam and early detection of SARS meant that many new cases were identified and isolated. Lives were saved. The virus, however, took his life. He knew he was dying. Dr. Scott Dowell, a WHO doctor who attended to Carlo in Bangkok, aptly said, "To be by yourself in a strange country, in a room full of people in spacesuits who cannot touch you... That is not a good way to die." Would you tell us about his emotions?*

– His last days will always be in my heart: not being able to communicate, the suffering; the thought of leaving his children; his telling me – even if with a slight movement – how deeply he loved us all. This is what I remember with so much agony.

– *Your loss was so sudden and unexpected; but his sacrifice helped safe thousands of lives. What is Carlo legacy to the world?*

– Carlo's legacy is in his teachings: anybody has the power to contribute to build a stable path to peace. This is not just silence of guns and weapons, but also the respect for poverty, dignity, and health.

§ HOW CARLO SAVED MY LIFE

By Christopher Yates *

Who is Carlo Urbani? I'll get to that.

We were sitting at an Internet café in Hoi An, Vietnam checking email and catching up on world events. The cloud cover and the dramatic dip in temperature were a welcome relief after several days of exploring the area in the heat of a midday sun. When I woke up the next I noticed that I had a tickle in the back of my nose. No big deal, I thought. But that night the tickle turned to a dry itch and by morning my eyes felt itchy and my nose began to run. No big deal, I thought, just a cold. I dug through our packs for some Echinacea we had acquired in South Africa and deliberately sought out a bowl of hot

* First published on April 9, 2003 as part of the special "Colleagues pay tribute to Carlo Urbani", Bangkok Post. Courtesy of Christopher Yates.

chicken soup.

Although I had developed all the symptoms of a cold: sneezing, drippy nose, watery itchy eyes and a few body aches we still ran around Hoi An, visiting shops getting measured for custom tailored clothing and getting lost around town. It was the seventh of March. The weather continued to be overcast to match my mood as I grew weaker and weaker. Although it had cooled down considerably Lisa noticed that I was sweating a lot. We unfolded our impressive backpackers medical kit and put our digital thermometer to use. It was official. I had a fever.

Convinced I was suffering from a cold, I remained in bed for the next two days and Lisa ferried food to me at regular intervals, even managing to forage for some hot Lasagna from our favorite Italian food place in town. Sometimes a cold is just a cold I told myself.

By March 10 my fever had been going up and down for three days. Somewhere in my mind was another thought, one so dark that I kept trying to push it to the corner of my fevered imagination. I might have malaria or some other god awful tropical disease. The thought was there but lurking at a distance like a wild animal circling a camp fire, wanting to attack but held back by the light. We had just spent four weeks in malarial areas of Northern Thailand, Laos, Cambodia and Southern Vietnam. I was also losing weight quicker than a Jenny Craig spokes-model, having lost 20 pounds since we had left Northern

Thailand on Feb 12th, 26 days earlier. We talked about our options for almost ten seconds and decided to throw in the towel. We needed to get me to a hospital.

We cancelled our plan to visit Hue by train and to endure another 13-hour train ride to Hanoi several days later. On March 11 Lisa tried really hard to help me have a good birthday by buying me a one-way airplane ticket to Hanoi the next day. Lisa took good care of me and the words "...in sickness and in health..." still echo through my head as she cared for me and told me how much she loved me. I still felt like &*#%!

Through the night I continued to have hot flashes but surprisingly no chills. I had some bad dreams. I was exhausted but the sniffling, sneezing, stuffy head, itchy eye headaches had passed during the night which gave me a false sense of recovery. Unfortunately my chest was now bearing the burden. I had a dry hacking cough as I forced full lungs of air through my throat to clear some invisible collection of phlegm. I had developed the much-dreaded unproductive cough. My temperature continued to fluctuate between 99.0 and 100.4. One hundred and forty days on the road and memories of the comforts of home seemed like a distant dream of the land of milk and honey.

We packed up our massive collection of silk purses, dresses, shirts, silk lanterns and other souvenirs and had the guest house arrange a cab to the airport 30 km north in Danang. It was the fifth day I was sick and although I was convinced I had malaria I felt strangely energized with the relief that we were going to do something about it.

So who is Carlo Urbani?

I'm getting to that.

We arrived at the Hanoi airport and after the regular hassles of collecting bags, arranging transport to the city center and locating a hotel, we packed our vaccination cards and sterile hypodermic needles into Lisa's purse and ordered another taxi.

Our guesthouse counter person advised us to go to the best hospital in Hanoi, which turned out to be the Vietnam-France Hospital. We agreed that the best in Hanoi would have to be good enough. "To the Vietnam-France Hospital", we ordered our taxi driver and into the sunset we drove.

This is where things started getting really weird. We pulled up to the hospital gate and it was closed. The taxi driver spoke to the guard while we waited for the gates to swing open and the angels of mercy to extend their healing arms to us. We noticed a whole lot of people dressed in surgical gowns and wearing facemasks wandering around outside the hospital but inside the gate. It must be break time I thought.

Suddenly the guard was at our window and he asked us what we wanted. That's a dumb question I thought. "I need to see a doctor" I exclaimed with as much authority as I could muster. The guard didn't hesitate as he looked me in the eye and said, "The hospital is closed." I was stunned. Surely this man had confused his native Vietnamese translation into English. We protested our right to access and the guard exerted his power to deny it to us. He produced a letter protected by a clear sheet of acetate and handed it to me. It certainly looked official. Sure enough, it said the hospital was closed.

My initial reaction when I saw the words was disbelief. Who closes a hospital? I mean, really, throw me a fricken bone here people! I could see what appeared to be doctors just mulling around, some lifting their masks to take a drag from their lit cigarettes. I scrutinized the letter and marveled at the official looking letterhead. I read on: "The hospital has been closed for one week for annual disinfecting." I looked back up at the pale green-gowned staff caged like animals behind the wrought-iron fence. Something was not right. No one closes a modern hospital in a developing nation!! ....unless...........Oh!!.........The thought struck Lisa and I simultaneously and we looked at each other with big eyes. Maybe there's been an outbreak of something. Our boiling frustration instantly melted away to be replaced by confusion and relief.

We backed down on our demand and consulted our ragged guidebook hoping there was an alternative. SOS International, a private medical evacuation clinic, was near the city center. The clinic would be set up to get us to Singapore quickly for modern medical treatment facilities if it turned out I had come down with some dreaded tropical disease. We asked the taxi driver to take us there and he backed away from the gates and melted into the mass of traffic towards the city center. I did not feel feverish as we climbed the steps to the clinic. Once inside the air-conditioned clinic we were relieved to find a very clean and professional medical office. After the obligatory filling out of the papers I was sitting shirtless answering questions posed to me by an expert in tropical infectious diseases. The visit alone was a huge relief.

After taking my temperature and listening to my cough for an abnormally long amount of time, the doctor asked which countries we had been to. "How do I answer that one" I wondered. "Let's see...Kenya, Tanzania, Zimbabwe, Botswana, Namibia, South Africa, Lesotho, Mauritius, Malaysia, Thailand, Burma, Laos, Cambodia and Vietnam". Each had its own collection of nasty little bugs. I was impressed with myself and of our adventure thus far. Unimpressed, the doctor asked the pointed question, "Have you traveled to Hong Kong or China?"

"No, not yet" I replied. It seemed an odd question at the time. I would assume there would be more risk of catching some dreadful tropical disease in Cambodia or Laos or Botswana or Burma. A few more deep breathes with a cold stethoscope face pressed to my back. "So you haven't been to Hong Kong or China?" I stuck to my guns with an emphatic "No". I put on my shirt as the doctor sifted through the evidence in her head. She collected herself and sat motionless as she delivered her conclusion.

My blood should be tested for dengue fever but my fever pattern didn't match that of malaria. If the fever returned in the next day, she advised, come back in immediately and she would test my blood for the malaria parasite. Otherwise it looked as if I just had a case of the Asian flu. She didn't bother to tell us why travel to Hong Kong or China was relevant and we didn't bother to ask.

Ten minutes later I was lying on an examination bench in an immaculate clinic with a needle slowly piercing my skin in search of a vein. We had purchased a medical kit in London that included various sized hypodermic needles and syringes and for good measure we insisted on using our paraphernalia. It was all the same to the phlebotomist who took sadistic pleasure in pulling a length of surgical hose tight around my arm and searching for a bulging vein. I was surprised to learn that the test for dengue fever would only take ten minutes.

We were relieved to hear that dengue fever was not the culprit. I didn't even know what dengue fever was when I was lying in a pool of my sweat back in Hoi An. A curious result of my blood test revealed blood platelet counts below normal levels. But rest and fluids would supposedly provide the remedy. We paid an outrageous sum of money for the clinic visit and retreated to our mini-hotel to suffer a night of midnight motorbike madness in the old quarter of Hanoi.

The next day while "taking it easy" in an Internet café we learned of the whole story of how the mystery virus SARS had brought the entire Vietnam-France Hospital in Hanoi to its knees.

So who is Carlo Urbani?

If SARS was an invisible infectious cloud blowing out of southern China, Urbani was the canary in its path.

Carlo Urbani was the director of infectious diseases for the Western Pacific Region of the World Health Organization (WHO). He was called to the bedside of Johnny Chen, an American businessman who came to the Vietnam-France hospital on February 26 with flulike symptoms that quickly deteriorated into pneumonia and fever, as well as dry cough. The hospital initially suspected that he had the Asian "bird flu" that killed a bunch of people in 1997. Rumors of a mystery pneumonia had been coming out of Southern China but the Chinese authorities had been tight lipped, even instructing local news reporters to ignore it. Before he died, Chen had infected 80 people, including more than half of the health workers who cared for him. His infections was traced back to the Metropole hotel in which he stayed on the same floor as a 64 year old doctor from Guangdong in southern China (where they think the virus originated).

Working in the French hospital in Hanoi, Carlo Urbani witnessed the SARS virus infect one nurse after another. He quickly realized the disease was highly contagious. He took unprecedented steps to warn the world of the danger, and then in a twist of prophetic irony, he died.

On March 9, Urbani and other WHO specialists pleaded with the Vietnam Health Minister to isolate patients, screen travelers, and to seriously consider closing the Vietnam-France Hospital in Hanoi. Because Urbani had a great deal of credibility with the Vietnamese government and with dozens of health care workers at the hospital sick, on March 11, my Birthday, the Vietnam Health Minister ordered the hospital closed. We arrived at the hospital gates less than 24 hours later. Urbani's quick action was later credited with shutting down Vietnam's first outbreak.

On March 11, Urbani traveled to Bangkok for a conference on de-worming school children. But he wasn't feeling well. He was taken to a hospital where he began to feel better within several days but he had watched this play out before and he admitted to colleagues that he was scared. He ordered himself isolated and a special room was built for him. With personal connections to WHO specialists, several flew in to help him. Patches soon showed up on x-rays of his lungs and a few days later as his lungs began to weaken he was put on a respirator. As fluid filled his lungs he was put on a more powerful respirator and sedated with morphine. The end came at 11:45 on Saturday morning, March 29, 18 days after realizing he was coming down with the symptoms himself. Carlo Urbani was 46 years old.

With many of the hospital staff ill, our visit a day earlier would have certainly exposed both Lisa and I to massive doses of the virus. At the very least we would have been stuck in Vietnam under quarantine. It is very sad that to raise awareness as he did, he had to pay such a price. There is little doubt in my mind that Carlo Urbani's quick action and resolve may have saved my life.

For that I thank you. God Bless you and your family, Dr. Urbani.

§ HEROES AND HEROINES OF THE WAR ON SARS

By Chee Yam Cheng *

On 12 March 2003, the World Health Organization (WHO) issued a worldwide alert about the severe acute respiratory syndrome (SARS). The rapidly progressive, sometimes-fatal atypical pneumonia appeared to have risen in Guangdong in Southern China. Singapore was already one of the countries with known SARS cases, together with China, Hong Kong, Vietnam and Canada. By the end of March 2003, there were more than 1,600 cases and more than 50 deaths in over 12 countries.

As at 14 April, the situation had worsened. Newsweek reported the following statistics around the world –

---

* Dr. Chee Yam Cheng is *Senior Consultant and Clinical Professor, Department of General Medicine, Tan Tock Seng Hospital. He is Chairman Medical Board, Tan Tock Seng Hospital. Courtesy of the* Journal of the Singapore Medical Association, 2003.

country, number of cases/number of deaths as follows: Canada 74/7, USA 115/0, Ireland 1/0, UK 4/0, Belgium 1/0, France 3/0, Spain 1/0, Italy 3/0, Germany 5/0, Romania 1/0, Switzerland 1/0, China 1,220/49, Hong Kong 800/20, Taiwan 17/0, Thailand 7/2, Vietnam 59/4, Malaysia 1/1, Singapore 101/6 and Australia 1/0.

SARS is an infectious disease with the coronavirus as its cause. There are documented primary, secondary and tertiary cases and even worse, community cases where tracing the SARS contact has become impossible. SARS has spread throughout the world because people can be exposed in one area and be on the other side of the world a day later when they take ill.

In the New England Journal of Medicine issue dated 31 March 2003, three articles on SARS were published. The titles were A Cluster of Cases of SARS in Hong Kong, Identification of SARS in Canada and an Editorial, Case Clusters of the SARS. They described 10 cases each in Hong Kong and Toronto. On 2 April 2003, the New England Journal of Medicine editorial was titled "Faster ...but Fast Enough?" Responding to the epidemic of SARS and on 7 April, the same journal published "A Major Outbreak of SARS in Hong Kong" which analysed 138 cases in the Prince of Wales Hospital.

On 10 April, the same journal had two articles. The first was "Identification of a Novel Coronavirus in Patients with SARS," by the group in Germany (where our Singaporean doctor was warded) and the other "A Novel Coronavirus

Associated with SARS" by members of the SARS working group which included our Microbiologist Dr Ling AE of Singapore General Hospital and Dr Carlo Urbani. Dr Urbani succumbed to SARS and the latter article was dedicated to the memory of him.

Carlo Urbani

Dr Urbani was a 46-year-old WHO physician and infectious disease specialist whose work defined SARS. He died in Thailand on 29 March 2003 of SARS – a valiant fallen hero in the battle against SARS. The members of the SARS working group proposed that the novel coronavirus be named the Urbani SARS – associated coronavirus.

His involvement goes back to Hanoi, when he was called in as an epidemiological expert to examine patients at the Vietnam-French Hospital there. He alerted the world to the disease. Without the early warning by him, the outbreak could have been worse. He was an Italian WHO epidemiologist at the WHO office in Hanoi who first responded to anxious hospital officials who reported to him that a sick Chinese American businessman (Mr Johnny Cheng) was infecting doctors and nurses with a strange pneumonia. He visited the hospital daily and first treated Mr Cheng on 26 February. Over the next week, Dr Urbani was in the hospital taking samples and working with staff there, who themselves started to get sick. And then Dr Urbani himself got sick. It was Dr Urbani who recognised that health workers were being infected by close contact with patients and alerted health authorities that infection control safeguards were essential. WHO credited him with alerting the world to the need for heightened global surveillance for the disease and for bringing the SARS outbreak under control in Hanoi.

Many healthcare workers at the Hanoi hospital took ill, several critically so. Health officials therefore shut it down and imposed a quarantine. Dr Urbani, already ill was airlifted to a Bangkok hospital where despite treatment, he died. He was in 1999 the President of the Italian branch of Medicins Sans Frontiers and accepted the Nobel Peace Prize on behalf of the relief aid group. He was an expert in parasitic diseases of school children and had worked in Cambodia, Laos and Vietnam. As a young man of 22, he had left his hometown of Maiolati Spontini near Ancona on Italy's Adriatic coast to work among African communities.

His philosophy was this. "Health and dignity are indissociable in human beings. It is a duty to stay close to victims and guarantee their rights." In Hanoi he stayed close to the victims of the disease until he himself took ill and died. To the Bangkok team, Dr Urbani is a hero. Health care workers around the world may owe their lives to his recognition of the need for stringent protections, although that recognition came too late to save him.

"This is a much more serious illness than many people, including some health officials, appreciate. It is dramatically more severe than other diseases that are spread by the same route. People need to recognise that more needs to be done. Otherwise, I fear SARS is gong to be with us for a long time," Dr Scott Dowell said. (Dr Dowell, from the Centre for Disease Control and Prevention in Atlanta, is director of a programme set up to detect new diseases in Asia and is based in Bangkok.)(9)

Hanoi Heroes and Heroines

When Dr Carlo Urbani investigated the outbreak at the Vietnam-France Hospital in Hanoi, he met with a dedicated team of healthcare workers there who were treating Vietnam's only index patient – a 48-year-old Chinese-American businessman, Johnny Cheng, who first brought the disease to the country after having visited Shanghai and Hong Kong. He had fallen ill in Hanoi and was put on artificial respiration on 2 March and died on 13 March in a Hong Kong hospital. Events snowballed from there. Some days earlier, some of the staff began to complain of shivers and headaches. They were hospitalised and then the hospital was closed. Local companies refused to deliver food to the hospital. A support committee was formed to bring in meals and other aid. They were locked up with the beast. Draconian hygiene measures were put in place. But two nurses and two doctors died. Said Dr Vu Hoang Thu, "We were very scared. But we did not have a choice, we had to work, to care for our colleagues. Those who were in good health saw others falling sick and their health deteriorate. We cried a lot. But we had to encourage them; and for some, lie to them about the progress of the illness. What we lived through, it was like a war. Without force, without solidarity, we would not have been able to get through it"(10).

So when the deadly SARS virus sweeping the world hit this Hanoi hospital, doctors and staff decided to lock themselves away with the killer virus to prevent it escaping into the wider community. Thanks to their quick action, the outbreak was contained but four health care workers died.

Singapore Battlefield

On 22 March 2003, Tan Tock Seng Hospital (TTSH) was declared the dedicated SARS hospital for Singapore. All SARS cases, suspect and probable as defined by the WHO case criteria, were isolated at Tan Tock Seng Hospital. All other hospitals and clinics where patients were seen and SARS diagnosed were to have them transferred to TTSH. However, many of the frontlines of battle were also out there in the primary care clinics.

It was on 29 March 2003 that following a symposium organised by the College of Family Practitioners and the Ministry of Health that the "Interim Advisory on SARS for doctors practising in primary care and family practice settings in Singapore" was issued. It was updated subsequently on 3 and 12 April. The College SARS Workgroup was spearheading this effort to equip our frontline doctors with knowledge, skills and protective gear. Should they encounter any case in their clinics, they were to suitably protect themselves and their clinic staff before examining the patient and then referring the latter to TTSH via a private ambulance service.

So while there was much focus on TTSH and the work of its staff, "GPs deserve praise and government help too". So was the title of a letter to the Straits Times forum page on 17 April 2003(11). She wrote, "While the Tan Tock Seng Hospital doctors and nurses rightfully deserve the cheesecakes, roses and accolades piled on them, let us not forget the unsung heroes, the humble general practitioner (GP) and his clinic assistants. No less at the front line, they face increasing isolation as they grapple with a falling patient load and increase in overheads (masks, bleaches and antiseptic washes don't come any cheaper to them) amid fears that they themselves may become infected by SARS".

Hospital Doctors and Nurses

Although TTSH is the designated SARS hospital, it is obvious that all healthcare workers from doctors down to the cleaners are at risk of contracting the disease in the workplace in the other hospitals and clinics. Some problems were acutely faced by staff of TTSH. So I would like to be specific to TTSH but at the same time not lose sight of the issues affecting all health care workers working outside of TTSH.

Nurses faced the unknown when the SARS outbreak began. On 12 March when the first SARS case was reported in Singapore (the first index case was admitted to Tan Tock Seng Hospital on 1 March) no one knew how the virus spread, much less how patients should be treated. Within two weeks a system was in place that involved "gowning up" and showering before leaving the hospital. Uniforms would be left at the hospital for disinfection. Said a nursing officer, "It was unbearable to see patients suffering. And it was crushing to lose any to SARS. What was worse, many of those falling victims to the disease were colleagues. However internal support was very strong. We would buy each other gifts and chocolates to cheer each other up"(12).

What made it especially difficult were the prejudices nurses faced. Taxis and even buses refused to stop at the hospital. Neighbours did not want to ride the lift with them. At any packed food court, there would always be a seat for a TTSH nurse. Queue lines would quickly shorten when a nurse joined that queue. Then came the outpouring of tributes to these healthcare workers on the SARS frontline. Taxis began showing up at the hospital. Other hospitals sent their nurses to help out at TTSH – 18 from the Singapore General Hospital and two from Alexandra Hospital. To our nurses, patients come first. They deliver care to them regardless of the disease they have. They are not quitting.

In support of the critical roles nurses play, one writer to the forum page said, "Saying thanks is fine, but let us pay our nurses more"(13). It is one thing to express gratitude and thanks to the healthcare staff who care for patients with SARS. But he said: "What Singaporeans have mistakenly identified as "exceptional courage" in nurses is in fact an inherent personality trait. Their capacity for love, sympathy and endurance, unfazed by the fatal experience of their fellows, defines who they truly are; tending to the sick and suffering in what they do. It is more than just a job or a passion. It is the conviction of their calling. This is their creed.... Their hospital workplace is a battlefield of germs, and the SARS virus is merely the latest, though not the deadliest, to enjoin the daily battles". He went on to extol, "They perform their tasks with effortless cheer, as they fight the bugs to the end with every trick, knowledge and passion to make a difference to the comfort of the sick and unwell. Unknown to many, the nurse is also the doctor's guard against forgetfulness, his ever-present and questioning conscience; at times, she is his challenge and often, his skilled right arm". His conclusion? "We need to reward our nurses more, to demonstrate the sincerity of our messages of gratitude and thanks, failing which the Courage Fund and the compliments would be just empty symbols."

On the other side of the coin, the President of the Health Corporation of Singapore Staff Union had this to say: "We are the union representing more than 5,000 workers in the restructured hospitals in Singapore. The last four weeks have been trying for healthcare workers and their families. The union is extremely proud that the healthcare workers have risen to the occasion. They have gone beyond the call of duty to combat and contain disease.

Recently incidents have been reported of healthcare workers being shunned by some members of the public. We understand the public's anxieties for their safety and that of their families.... We are very touched by the kind words and gestures from the members of the public. On behalf of all the healthcare workers in Singapore, we would like to say "Thank You" to all of you."

What about our doctors? Big sacrifices... behind doctors' masks(14). Bound by the Hippocratic Oath and The Physician's Pledge of the Singapore Medical Council, TTSH doctors said fighting the unknown virus as well as fighting discrimination from the public and sometimes even their own families, had been worth it. Behind 'the masks' they had to deal with a lot of personal pain and sacrifices. One doctor had to stay with a colleague because his parents kicked him out of the family home. Another lived separately from wife and child, just to be safe. Another said his brother's colleagues avoided him because he is working at TTSH. Yet others have began sorting out their financial arrangements, in particular their insurance policies and wills. What boosts their morale? It is the messages of gratitude and encouragement from relatives of patients and even strangers.

Illness Made Public

It was in the news that one of our fellow colleagues took ill in New York in mid-March and was quarantined and hospitalised in Frankfurt when he was en route home to Singapore. Both he and his wife and motherin-law were reported in the medical journal as cases from whom clinical samples were taken and from which a novel coronavirus was identified(7). In this article our doctor colleague is the index patient, his wife (also a doctor) is contact one and contact two is the mother of contact one. Our colleague had treated a patient with atypical pneumonia who had arrived from Hong Kong and was warded at TTSH on 1 March 2003. From 3 to 9 March, our colleague treated her, then left for New York to attend a medical conference. His illness began when he was in New York and on 13 March he flew home but during the stopover in Frankfurt, Germany all three were transferred to an isolation unit with suspected SARS.

Our gratitude to him and his family must be for the samples they provided to the German doctors at the Frankfurt University Hospital. From there and yet other samples as reported in the publication(7), a sequence of 300 nucleotides in length was obtained by a polymerasechain reaction based random amplification procedure. Genetic characterisation of this coronavirus showed that it is only distantly related to known coronaviruses (identical in 50 to 60 percent of the nucleotide sequence).

Further downstream, this nucleotide sequence has resulted in the production of a diagnostic test kit which is undergoing clinical testing. As we know today, there are different parts of the virus from which primers have been made. There are three undergoing testing in Singapore and the German version called the Artus-Bernhard Nocht

Institute version would have had inputs from our Singaporean colleagues who happened to be their patients. The other kits are from CDC (Centre for Disease Control, Atlanta) and GIS (Genome Institute of Singapore).

SERGIO VIEIRA DE MELLO

Matthew Couper
Sergio Vieira de Mello
2011
Pencil on paper
7" x 5" / 175mm x 135
mmwww.mattcouper.com

Sérgio Vieira de Mello

de Mello

1948

~ 1948 august

2003

24 years with United Nations

Matthew Cooper 2011

"He represented the very highest standards of service to the international community and mankind. He dedicated his life to serving others, seeking to alleviate their suffering and repair their broken dreams."

— *Jimmy Carter*
Former US President (1977-1981)

§ A WORLD OF DIGNITY

By Sergio Vieira de Mello *

I am delighted to be here tonight to give this third lecture on world civilization. I am also terrified. These impressive surroundings, my more than impressive audience which includes, so I understand, another room full of students whose reactions I will not be able to gauge (how terrifying is that?), as well as the humble topic of world civilization, conspire to make this a rather intimidating occasion.

But it is also an occasion that I jumped at the chance to be part of. The subject matter and this forum give me an opportunity to speak with a latitude and a frankness that rarely comes my way. The carefully choreographed world

* Text of the Third Annual BP World Civilisation Lecture, delivered by Sergio Vieira de Mello – then United Nations High Commissioner for Human Rights – at the British Museum, London, on November 11, 2002.

249

of diplomacy certainly has its place: it provides a structure for engagement and dialogue that is designed (or so the theory goes) to minimize the risk of being misunderstood. Equally, however, that framework can be muzzling in its effect: the room for frank tour d'horizons is very limited. Tonight is different.

Which is not to say, of course, that I am hoping to be misunderstood.

Today's date and all that it signifies provides a reference point that is both too obvious and too important to ignore. It is fitting that this lecture should take place on Remembrance Day, as we honour those who died in the First World War: the war, I need hardly add, that was supposed to end all wars. If we are to discuss world civilisation, whatever that may mean, it is important that we remember those who have suffered as a result of a breakdown of civilisation. We must also pay tribute to – and think, really think hard of – the women, men and children who continue to suffer the impact of armed conflict.

By conservative estimates, some eight million men, women and children died in The Great War. Countless others were wounded, imprisoned, displaced or disappeared. Millions more were scarred by this horror, a horror that occurred among what are viewed as being some of the pre-eminent civilisations of the time.

The international community resolved, at the end of the

War, to never again allow such human devastation. Governments banded together to establish the League of Nations, an organization dedicated to promoting international cooperation and achieving peace and security.

Many consider the League to have been unsuccessful. They consider it so because it failed to prevent the outbreak of the Second World War, which was a conflict – to the extent these comparisons have any meaning – still more terrible than the First.

Yet it remains a fact that its creation did see the emergence of a deeper appreciation and awareness of human dignity and the sanctity of human life, as well as of the world's growing inter-connectedness. It laid the foundation for the establishment of the United Nations and paved the way for the international protection of human rights. It is a source of pride to me that the Office I arrived at only two months ago is called the Palais Wilson, the original home of the League of Nations. "Wilsonianism" is a concept that is frequently derided as being either naïve or a failure, or both: I disagree entirely with the former and only partially with the latter.

In short, it would be wrong to underestimate the importance of valuing these post-War achievements. It would be difficult to imagine the establishment today of a similar framework for attempting to ensure peace, security and respect for human rights, such as the UN system, if these institutions did not already exist. And that really is a question to ponder on (and one to which I will not attempt an answer): would the world we live in today have the capacity and the vision to create a United Nations as pure in its ideals as the one established in 1945? What would the world look like today had the United Nations not existed? It is fortunate that we do not have to answer these questions for real.

In the post-War years the international community committed to a set of basic universal values: equality, dignity, tolerance and non-discrimination. We recognised, through the Universal Declaration of Human Rights, that "the inherent dignity and the equal and inalienable rights of all members of the human family is the foundation of freedom, justice and peace in the world". "Freedom from fear and want" was our common aspiration. And we agreed, in words of truly elemental passion and force, that "we the peoples" would be "determined to save succeeding generations from the scourge of war". Together, we created a set of international human rights standards rooted firmly in these values and goal.

Yet we have failed in our duties to ensure that these standards are upheld. Too often our world excludes and marginalises those of its citizens who, as a result of violence, inequality, intolerance, discrimination, are incapable of participating in any meaningful way, and worse: who have misery upon misery heaped on them.

I hope you do not think me a coward but civilisation is, I would suggest, a concept that eludes definition. You will not get one from me. I acknowledge that this is a problem in terms of academic rigour for I shall be using the word "civilisation" often in my address, but a definition risks being either pretentious or subjective or incomplete, or a combination of these failings. And I must confess I am even more sceptical of attempting a definition of "world civilisation", which for me has rather alarming connotations of pan-uniformity. The best I can do is, first, to suggest that we should eschew homogeneity and embrace difference; and, secondly, to suggest that focusing on common perceptions of human dignity may be more fruitful than the pursuit of one world civilisation.

Furthermore, the difficulty of obtaining a satisfactory definition should not be used, or should not be allowed, to obfuscate the picture. For what I can tell you is that I know what is uncivilised: I have seen it. We all know. In my work with the United Nations, most of which I have spent in what we in peaceful and prosperous countries refer to euphemistically as "the field", I have seen not only the best but also the worst of what we have to offer each other. Such behaviour can be found everywhere. As a UN worker I have had to pause and wonder how different societies can develop such ruthless disregard for human life.

Common perceptions of "civilization" have largely positive connotations. They suggest both a moral milieu as well as the attainment of some sort of cultural summit: they evoke images of arts and culture, of enlightenment, of sophistication (indeed, images of which all the very things contained in this amazing building are an embodiment).

They suggest evolution (in a non-biological sense) or progress in social development.

But I would suggest that the term civilization risks (but by no means implicitly carries) worryingly negative notions. And these are notions of cultural superiority, of elitism, of imperialism and – largely speaking – of Western idealism. If one considers oneself civilised, after all, then those who are different are not civilised: they are uncivilised. Indeed, it was only a few years ago that it was suggested that western concepts were so dominant, so incontrovertibly accepted, that what we were witnessing was an "end of history" in the sense that there was no longer the fuel for a clash of civilisations. Who would really dare propound such hubristic notions now?

We must also acknowledge that the word "civilisation" has been used throughout the course of history to justify brutality, expansionist thinking and behaviour, colonialism, even slavery and genocide, as in my continent, the Americas. In carrying out these acts, these civilisations argued that they were, in fact, on "civilising" missions. Our discussion of world civilization must bear these facts in mind.

Some might argue that at the start of this new millennium we have achieved world civilization: that is, an advanced stage of social development at the global level – a contemporary version, so to speak, of Hegel's Weltgeist, the spirit of the world. It is true that we live in an era of unprecedented wealth and of extraordinary technological, scientific and educational advancement. The world is more democratic today than ever before: 140 countries now hold multiparty elections. The number of inter-state wars, and of the human lives lost as a result of those wars, has dropped considerably. Global markets have opened up as the result of new technology and increased economic integration has helped to create new opportunities. Globalization has created the potential for greater communication and exchanges between different cultures. In so doing it has paved the way for greater human freedom.

But in spite of these many positive developments, the end of the Cold War (now often treated almost with nostalgia by some) and the continuing process of globalisation have also given rise to many uncertainties. New forms of terrorism have emerged, creating untold suffering recently in New York, in Bali, and in Moscow. The human costs of terrorism have been felt equally in the Philippines, the Middle East, Algeria and Sri Lanka, just as they have been felt – in years now thankfully receding – in many countries of Western Europe. Internal armed conflicts continue to ravage countries around the world: who here is not tempted – though we would be wrong to do so – to throw their hands up in despair when the Democratic Republic of the Congo or Colombia are mentioned?

Seemingly intractable global conditions such as poverty, HIV/AIDS, racism and gender inequality continue to cause widespread human misery. These conditions contribute to the growing marginalization of individuals and communities and, where left unaddressed, create tensions, jeopardize human development and threaten security. Allow me to address some of these issues in more detail, for each one of them constitutes the antithesis of civilization.

Although international wars have decreased in number, *internal conflicts* have killed about 3.6 million people over the last decade. Particularly worrying is the increasing victimization of civilians: more than 90% of those injured or killed in post-cold war conflicts have been civilians, and half of these were children. The number of refugees and internally displaced people has risen sharply, an indication of the increased intensity – by which I mean disregard for the non-combatant – of today's conflicts.

Extreme poverty marginalises around 1.5 billion people and continues to hamper international efforts towards sustainable human development. Although the world has adequate food resources to feed the entire population, every week thousands of children die from malnutrition-related diseases before their first birthday, and thousands more suffer from stunted growth.

While some gains have been made, poverty remains acute and pervasive in many countries. Those affected are among those most vulnerable to deterioration in their living conditions through low nutrition, exclusion from education, justice and housing, lack of adequate health care, and restrictions on their privacy and personal security. In short, the poor are deprived of the basic freedoms that are fundamental for minimal human dignity. This is appalling, not least when we consider the wealth available worldwide. The richest 1% of people in the world receive as much income each year as the poorest 57%. This is not an indictment of the 1% but it is an indictment of the denial of opportunity for the 57%.

Diseases such as *HIV/AIDS* are crippling many of the same communities that shoulder the burden of poverty. The scale of the AIDS epidemic has far exceeded even the worst scenarios predicted a few years ago and countries of the South continue to bear the brunt: 90% of the 40 million people living with HIV/AIDS are in developing countries. The epidemic is decimating societies in sub-Saharan Africa where, in countries such as Botswana, 40% of all adults are affected. HIV/AIDS strikes those in the most productive years of their life and, in some areas, is depleting a generation of mothers, of teachers, of law-enforcement officials and of health care providers. It is also producing a generation of orphans who are particularly vulnerable to discrimination, exploitation and abuse. And the virus is spreading with recent reports predicting its imminent explosion in Eurasia.

This is a humanitarian and social disaster of historic proportions, one which exacts a staggering human toll, derails economic opportunities and blocks development prospects. It is, above all, an affront to the human rights of those infected and affected, who are marginalised and excluded. Yet the economic and political response to this crisis has been achingly slow and inadequate, in spite of the fact that HIV/AIDS is now both preventable and treatable.

Racism and intolerance. This blight persists in virtually every corner of the globe. The situation is arguably worsening: the resurgence of anti-Semitism, including in Western Europe, as well as the rise of the new and disturbing phenomenon of vilifying Islam, are particularly worrying and, alone, pose serious questions to any defenders there may be of the concept of a world civilization. Intolerance, as one its many evils, is rarely honest about its motives: it hides behind many pretexts. Protecting human rights is first and foremost the responsibility of States. Yet governments have been too passive in tackling different recent manifestations of intolerance and, in fact, often contribute to them.

Gender: Many of the profound political, social and economic changes that have characterized the past decade or so have impacted negatively on women. The traumatic effects on women of conflict and human displacement are exacerbated by sexual violence. Economic instability and change hamper progress in the achievement of gender equality, notably due to the feminization of poverty. Institutional discrimination against women – in particular occupational discrimination and segregation – along with negative gender stereotypes persist in virtually all societies.

This situation is absurd. Not just because of the denial of fundamental rights it entails for women. But also because of the untapped advantages for us all that we are denied. Women are a force for peace. They are invariably the glue that binds families and communities, and they are the reconcilers. They are economic providers and, in many places, they are in the majority. To have them effectively silenced – to have women not participating fully in the shaping of their societies – makes no sense.

These problems are not necessarily new. Human beings have lived with war, disease and inequality for centuries. What is different today is that we have no excuse to be unaware of the divide between the world's rich and poor, the powerful and powerless, the included and marginalised. We cannot today justify claiming ignorance of the cost that this divide imposes on the poor and dispossessed while at the same time claim we have attained civilisation. In spite of this, too often we appear to surrender in the face of global challenges.

There is, or so it can seem, a palpable lack of empathy towards those affected: a dulling of critical analysis of policies that may impact communities and societies outside and beyond our own. But more than that, I suspect there is a dulling of our ability to appreciate what this impact may mean, in real terms, on those affected. The danger in assuming that we, the so-called international community, are "civilized" is this collective apathy to which we have become accustomed.

This cannot continue. We can no longer act as if only what happens in our immediate communities matters, as if we only owe solidarity to those within our neighbourhood, city or country. We should nurture our sense of self as part of a common humanity. We should appreciate better the ways in which we can all benefit from cooperation and solidarity across lines of nationality, gender, race or economic status. We should seize the potential of globalization to become a unifying and inclusive force: a globalization that places the promotion and protection of human rights at the heart of its objectives and strategies.

For human rights do indeed have a critical role to play today. In short, their indivisibility and universality are perhaps the closest concepts we have to being the foundations of a civilized world (as opposed to a world civilization).

The principles of social, political and economic inclusion are essentially based on rights and responsibilities. Those in positions of power and privilege, however, too often see rights and responsibilities, as a threat to their own interests. As a set of universally accepted values, principles and standards, which apply equally to all people, everywhere, human rights should in fact be seen as a tool to help build stable and prosperous communities.

I have made it clear that helping to foster the rule of law will be the overarching theme of my work as High Commissioner. The rule of law is the lynchpin of human rights protection: without it, respect for our dignity and for the equality and security of all human beings is meaningless.

Human rights work, in other words, is not just about morals or politics, but about responsibilities, legal obligations and accountability. Through the framework of the rule of law, human rights provide individuals with recourse when decisions are made which may adversely affect them: they also provide a means by which to attempt to ensure that those adverse decisions or actions are not taken in the first place. Rights aim to empower individuals by allowing us all to use them as leverage for action. They legitimize our voices, placing emphasis on the participation of individuals in decision-making. They seek to avoid discrimination through their equal application to us all.

Let us take the role of human rights in poverty reduction as an example. Poverty is defined by more than only a lack of income. Its dimensions include gender and racial discrimination, a lack of fundamental human rights such as education, health care, the components of an adequate living standard including nutrition and housing, and access to justice. Few of those living in extreme poverty can benefit from national institutions of accountability through which other citizens can claim their rights. It is unsurprising, then, that the poor often define the key dimension of poverty as being powerlessness.

Human rights principles and norms strengthen poverty reduction through the empowerment of poor people by expanding their freedom of choice and action to structure their own lives. A human rights approach looks behind national averages in order to identify the most destitute and vulnerable, and design initiatives to address their specific situations. It recognizes that all human beings should be entitled, based on principles of equality and dignity, to a set of minimum capabilities. These capabilities must be improved in order to overcome poverty. Human rights further strengthen what is now recognized as central to poverty reduction – the empowerment of the poor – by viewing the poor not as victims who need more resources, but as citizens who possess rights, and who are entitled to take part in decision-making in order to claim and exercise their rights.

I have been emphasising the need to ensure inclusivity and the participation of all members of society, and to ensure that marginalised and excluded groups have a meaningful voice. Effective human development can only be achieved where people are free to participate in the decisions that shape their lives. The free will of people to determine their own political, economic, social and cultural systems, and their full participation in all aspects of their lives, is something that to me is axiomatic. It is, in short, inherently "civilizing".

Democratic governance is based on the extension of civil and political rights: in particular the right to participate in political life. It is a basic form of organization or political order whose underlying principle is a recognition of the equal dignity and worth of every human being. Democracy provides the most appropriate framework for the realization of human rights. By allowing a voice in political decisions, it is instrumental in enabling us to realize other rights.

I do not suggest that democracy is the solution to all problems. It is vital to recognise and address democracy's shortcomings: democratic rule does not automatically correlate with respect for human rights, nor does its presence necessarily lead to economic and social development. The vast majority of democratic countries still limit important civil and political rights, and many often neglect economic and social rights, partly because this neglect is less obvious and does not hurt the electoral outcomes for those in power.

Countries in transition face particular challenges, as the replacement of an authoritarian regime with an electoral system does not solve existing human rights problems – on the contrary, many times the transition to a new order will bring to the surface a complex web of human rights issues. For example, just look at the challenges that were faced by South Africa, and which are currently being faced by East Timor, Sierra Leone and Afghanistan in figuring out how best to acknowledge the abuses that occurred in their recent pasts, break the cycle of impunity, and ensure that violence does not recur.

Democracies potentially face other weaknesses, as well. Democracy has been described as being, at its most crude, nothing more than allowing an individual a choice on one day in every four or so years. It has also been described as amounting to the tyranny of the majority.

Majority decision-makers may trample on the rights of minorities by excluding their participation, manipulating the media and political rights, setting aside the rule of law at the expense of minority rights in times of social upheaval, oppressing minority cultural practices, language and religion, and overriding minority economic interests all in pursuit of those interests held by the majority. Such dangerous utilitarianism sneak inside democracies: we should be alert to the risk.

Ironically, however, we should also take note of those *majorities* who are marginalized in many societies by the *minorities*. I am thinking here particularly of women and youths, as well as the least privileged.

Now, it is still overly simplistic to assert that full respect for human rights, democracy and the rule of law can prevent a meltdown of society. A civic order based on respect for human rights suggests that the authorities will respect individual rights. Governments, as I said, have the primary responsibility for the protection and promotion of human rights. But civic order also requires that the members of that polity, the citizens in some senses, will take on board their responsibilities towards each other.

This brings me to reflect on a relatively new concept of citizenship – since this is the BP lecture series – and that is the concept of corporate citizenship. If citizenship is, in effect, defined as the rights and duties of a member of a country, then companies, by extension, share those same rights and duties. It is no surprise, corporations being a collection of individual people, that their citizenship performance varies just as it does for any individual citizen.

As many of you know UN Secretary-General Kofi Annan launched the Global Compact over two years ago. In the very first principle, he asked companies to "support and respect the protection of international human rights within their sphere of influence". The citizenship performance of companies in this realm varies but thinking about the meaning of citizenship forces us all to consider the extent of our obligations and how best to meet them.

I come from a country famous for its rich cultural diversity – a country with more than 120 surviving indigenous nations and peoples, speaking even more indigenous languages and dialects. Peoples such as the Kayapo, Makuxi, Parakana, Xavante, Yanomami and many more have retained much of their culture and traditions, have strong attachments to their homelands: harvesting, managing and inter-relating within a space – the rainforests – that is also one of our planet's most important regions of biodiversity.

Mine is also a country that has pursued policies of development over decades and even centuries that have impinged upon and marginalized its original indigenous inhabitants. And if we look at recent years, we can say with some honesty that corporate Brazil – and I include international companies – has been one of the principal sources of the destruction not only of the forest itself but of the indigenous peoples' livelihoods and communities. We cannot say that Brazil has not made striking material advances but we must also acknowledge that indigenous peoples have been victims in many instances, rather than beneficiaries.

These observations lead me to a couple of comments. The first is related to what surprisingly is a relatively new phenomenon, at least in my region, namely that States are beginning to recognise that they are pluri-cultural and multiethnic. Our deeper Brazilian identity is rooted in our diverse cultures – our indigenous peoples, Afro-descendants and so on. No development however profitable should be undertaken at the expense of the rich cultural diversity to which I have referred, but rather for the benefit of all its components. Equality must be our goal.

Secondly, human rights are dynamic, not static. They move with the times. They confront new challenges. For indigenous peoples, the corporate sector presents such a new challenge with its technology, its apparently unlimited wealth and its legal expertise.

It is not easy to find the balance that will protect indigenous peoples rights, ensure the legitimate obligations of Governments towards all of their citizens, and not impede entrepreneurship and development. Some requirements are clear, however. Fair rules are important. Benefit-sharing is vital. The prior informed consent of the affected communities is an ideal towards which we should be aiming. You invited me to share some thoughts on the notion of civilization and my concept is one that includes indigenous peoples and their diverse cultures.

Let me turn to another changing conception of citizenship. While corporations are, through the conceptual framework of citizenship, being cast as world actors with specific responsibilities commensurate with their influence, at the same time individuals are increasingly voicing global rather than local concerns. There is recognition that we are part of a global community in which our actions impact life in other regions and that the concerns of others are also our concerns. While these might not always necessitate global solutions, these world-wide connections across frontiers are generating a sense of responsibility: not only within one's community but within empathetic networks across the world. This kind of interest and participation – what has been called "globalisation from below" – is vital to a healthy world civilization. Some moments ago, I condemned what I feared was something of a pervasive air of apathy in how, in general, looked on troubles experienced by those outside of our immediate frame of reference. This manifestation of globalisation provides some cause for optimism.

Now for the words you have been waiting to hear: In conclusion. What I am suggesting is that we may be overreaching ourselves to talk of world civilisation. We also may be misleading ourselves. More important than striving to attain such a state (or even to define it) is the need to focus on, highlight and better appreciate, the universality of human dignity. That, to me, would be a more productive avenue of investigation.

I have also tried to explain why I believe that human rights provide the best road map for this investigation. The principles of the UN Charter, the Universal Declaration and the other human rights instruments adopted in the last half-century are the closest we have to a universal code of conduct. These instruments provide the necessary building blocks to ensure that our common humanity is an inclusive one, built on values such as tolerance and dignity. The commitments they embody have been accepted voluntarily. It is the responsibility of all to ensure that they are respected.

Human rights possess a number of additional advantages of which we should be aware. First, they are easy to understand. Yet we have a tendency to engage in lengthy rarefied debates defining this right or that. Indeed, we do too much of this: the results are often, confusion, a degree of acrimony and the failure to implement the right in question. The victims, needless to say, have no problem in understanding what right it is that is being violated and how. Definitions and semantics have their role to play, for sure. Equally, they can provide foils for our failure to move forward.

Secondly, with rights come attendant responsibilities. Here I have offered some views on why it is not just states, primary though they are, but also others who must live up to their responsibilities in ensuring that our rights are respected.

It is also at the core of human rights that they apply to everyone. Inherent in them is a celebration of their universality as well as of diversity. Ensuring that we allow for such diversity and, by so doing, ensuring that we respect human rights, is my main message today. It is, I humbly suggest, a hugely relevant one. Ensuring that we allow for different cultures and people to co-exist and flourish alongside one another, is as current a priority today as it has ever been. Simply put, this is what civilisation may be all about.

§ IRAQ: THE UNITED NATIONS IS HERE FOR THE LONG HAUL

By IRIN News *

- *Iraq's Governing Council has finally met here in Baghdad. How significant a step do you believe this is for Iraq?*

- Well you heard me say a while ago that there are defining moments in history, and in my opinion in the history of Iraq this is one of those moments. Why? You heard me say that this is a unique situation for the Special Representative of the Secretary-General to have been appointed to a country that is a founding member of the organisation, but that is currently without a government and occupied by two other founding members of the

* Interview by IRIN (Integrated Regional Information Networks), part of the United Nations Office for the Coordination of Humanitarian Affairs. The interview was originally published on July 14, 2003, a little over a month before a truck bomb took the life of Sergio Vieira de Mello and members of his staff in Baghdad.

organisation that also happen to be Permanent Members of the Security Council.

This is bizarre, hence the importance of achieving what resolution 1483 calls for - which is an Iraqi interim administration as a first step towards an internationally recognised and representative government of Iraq, that will assume fully the sovereignty of this country. Now it is not for me to decide whether the General Council is the Iraqi Interim Administration, but I certainly see this as the first embodiment of an Iraqi executive authority which will fill this power vacuum that was making our work here extremely difficult in the absence of an Iraqi counterpart.

– You were closely involved with this. What exactly was your role in helping to put the new council together?

– Our role was to understand what the Iraqis expected from us. What they expected from us were two things. One, to help them convey a clear message to the coalition, particularly to Ambassadors Bremer and Sawers who were very receptive I must say - their aspiration that the council, whatever its name might be, would assume strong executive prerogative; and number two, that the United Nations would play a central role in the political and in the constitutional transition. And that is what we have tried to do with, I dare say, some success judging by today's (Sunday's) event.

– The UN Resolution 1483 says the interim body should be formed by the people of Iraq with the help of the authority

and working with the Special Representative. I have heard critics saying there should have been more meetings of ordinary people - and complaints that Iraqi exiles have been allowed to dominate. Do you think ordinary Iraqis who remained here have been involved enough?

– I can answer for myself and I have met with a broad section of Iraqis belonging to, what may be premature to call, a civil society, but still - professional groups - lawyers, journalists, doctors, professors, artists in addition to political and spiritual figures, and I believe that this governing council has been established with as much regard to the Iraqi civil society as was possible in the circumstances.

Number two: the reason why Ambassador Bremer changed the strategy midstream was precisely to help Iraqis form the Council that would be balanced in terms of internal and external representation. I hate the expression 'ethnic group' - but representation of different communities that form the Iraqi nation - religious and non-religious schools of thought and gender - even though admittedly three is too little, it is a beginning.

– The Americans are often perceived as unapproachable - do you see the UN's role as helping to bridge the divide between the coalition and the people? And do you feel Iraqis can really see the difference between the United Nations and the coalition.

– To the second question the answer is obviously yes - I think we must be honest to ourselves and recognise there exists in the minds of many Iraqis, mixed feelings about the record of the United Nations here and you can't expect them to make these fine distinctions between mandates given to the Secretary-General by the Security Council and the role of the Secretariat per se. They lump this all together as any public opinion would do - but they see clearly in the United Nations an independent and impartial player that is the only source of international legitimacy.

Hence the importance they attach to Resolution 1483, even though some complain that that resolution legitimised the occupation of Iraq. Hence the fact they invited me to speak this afternoon after the proclaimed creation of the Governing Council, presumably because they felt that was the only international voice required on that occasion.

Now as to our role - I would not describe it quite the way you did - what we have tried to do and will continue to do is to convey to the coalition and try to influence their thinking, based on what we gather as the aspirations of the Iraqi people. And I repeat, Ambassadors Bremer and Sawers have been quite open to that.

– Do you think you have more access to the Iraqi people being United Nations?

– I don't know if we have more access, but I believe they feel comfortable with us, they come here, they are in and out of this building. Sometimes we have to try to manage that because there are all kinds of visitors here, who are all welcome, needless to say, because this is their house, but who turn up unexpectedly without an appointment and want to see us and want to talk to us and express their frustrations, hopes etc. This is excellent, that is what we are here for.

And we then try to convey the gist of what we gather from all those contacts foreseen and unforeseen to the coalition, and we do the same in the provinces. Some religious leaders, such as Grand Ayatollah Sistani and also Samahat Sayyid al-Hakkim in Najaf, received us without any difficulty, whereas they may not be the same with others. So it all boils down to what I said earlier. We are seen to be independent, we are seen to be here to support them and achieve full self-government, that is full sovereignty, as soon as is possible.

– The Council will have the power to appoint ministers and approve the national budget and work with the Coalition on policies. But it is not clear if it can bring in new laws, for example, and Ambassador Bremmer retains the power of veto. Do you think the Council has been given enough power to do the job it needs to?

– Look, as compared to what we heard on arrival on 2 June what you saw today outlining the powers and prerogatives of the Governing Council, it's like night and day. Secondly, you also heard some of them this afternoon say that this is unfinished business. I'm speaking of definition of their authority. It will increase over time because I am convinced it is in the interest of the

Coalition to share as much power as authority - more than share, delegate as much authority and power to exercise it to the council as is possible. And this is an evolutionary process - it's an incremental one.

Whether the council will have legislative authority remains to be seen, I believe it will, because the only way of defining policies and of restoring law and order in a society is through legislation. Now even though they may not have legislative powers in a democratic sense, they are not elected, there may be a need to issue interim laws. You know in East Timor, we did not have this, apart from a Security Council resolution and we called them regulations, which at a later stage when a parliament, a legislature, is elected, will have to be either endorsed, confirmed, amended or appealed. My guess, although we haven't reached that stage yet, my guess is yes, you need laws to run the country.

– *The Americans were talking about a two-year plan to set up the council, appoint an advisory council on the constitution, draw it up, have a referendum and then have elections. Given your experience what will the United Nations' part be in all this - and do you think it is a realistic timetable?*

– I won't talk about a timetable, except to say a clear calendar is necessary and Ambassador Bremer and Ambassador Sawers have recognised that themselves, because the Iraqis need to feel that this transition is finite. How long that transition will last, I am not prepared to predict. What I know is that the United Nations is prepared, and I have said this to all Iraqis in the Governing Council as well as to other spiritual leaders and representatives of civil society that are not in Council, as I told the Coalition - the United Nations is prepared to help them implement and achieve whatever calendar and deadlines they will determine.

And if the Governing Council decides to establish a constitutional commission that will then make proposals to it as to what constitutional and electoral timetable should be, we are available to help them implement such a timetable. And I've also announced that a mission from the Electoral Assistance Division of our headquarters in New York will be coming to Baghdad later this month and will be available to advise the Governing Council on different options to achieve the ultimate goal which will be democratic, free and fair elections, and obviously the timetable will depend on the options they will choose.

– Do you think the council will help improve the security situation - is the unrest linked with Iraqis feeling they are not ruling themselves?

– I think it is a factor, so the mere creation of this Governing Council should send the message of confidence to the Iraqi people that they are retaking the reins of their destiny into their own hands. And secondly, it is also clear in the outline of their prerogative that the question of security, of police, of the new Iraqi army are within their remit. So they will be expected to play an active role in securing security fully in Iraq.

– *Are you satisfied with the speed of progress? You are half way into your term of office now.*

– The United Nations is here for the long haul - I am here for four months because I have another full-time job in Geneva that needs some attention, but I will be replaced, there will be continuity here.

– *You are going to report to the Security Council in less than two weeks - what will be the main thrust of your report? Are there particular areas you want to concentrate on?*

– The thrust will be the establishment of the Governing Council. Number two, as I told you, that depending on the wishes and choices of Iraqis, particularly the Governing Council, the United Nations should be ready to help them all the way, in whatever way we can, to organise the electoral process and to support the elaboration of a new constitution of Iraq.

Number three, that we should be available to assist all the new interim ministers, sector by sector, as the United Nations normally does through technical assistance, not least to bridge this huge gap that has been caused by the isolation and exclusion of Iraq. It is a knowledge gap. Help them update themselves with progress made, scientific, technological, managerial. Help them in making broad macro-economic financial and monetary decisions and help them restore, as it were, the civil administration capacity sector by sector.

In addition to that, we can also clearly play a role in the actual physical reconstruction of the country's infrastructure. But this will obviously very much depend on the outcome of the donor conference in October which we are actively preparing. And I should not forget, last but not least, all those initiatives that we can take very soon in the area of the promotion of human rights and true culture of democracy. One of those initiatives will be in the media sector, but also in a number of other areas related to human rights, to accountability for past crimes and the creation of a new justice system in Iraq, as well as the promotion of entire range of rights of Iraqi women. So that's a huge agenda, but there is no lack of commitment and determination on our part to achieve that.

§ MOURNING THE MAN, HONOURING THE MESSAGE

By Irene Khan *

The brutal murder of Sergio Vieira de Mello, Special Representative of the United Nations (UN) Secretary-General in Iraq, is yet more proof that people who serve humanity and defend human rights are easy targets in a world in which national security has trumped human security.

As the UN Special Representative in Iraq, he was a symbol of the international community's commitment to the country. As UN High Commissioner for Human Rights, Sergio was the highest authority on human rights in the world. This is a moment of deep grief for all those who care for Iraq and for human rights.

---

* Message from Irene Khan, Secretary-General of Amnesty International (AI Index: MDE 14/164/2003, News Service No: 194, 20 August 2003)

I mourn Sergio as a friend and as an international leader. He was a dynamo and a risk taker with great charm. He was a man of action and conviction, exuding all that is positive and passionate in life. But his death signifies much more than the passing of a good man.

The people of Iraq who believe in justice and peace are under attack. The international community is under attack. Human rights are under attack.

Sergio's murder has put at stake the fundamental human rights of the Iraqi people. It has put at risk the ability of the international community to stand with the Iraqi people in their struggle for human rights.

Sergio was convinced that the participation of all Iraqis was the foundation stone on which Iraq must be built. He championed the cause of human rights of Iraqis to those who did not want to hear.

If Sergio's death is to have any meaning, Iraq must be a building site for human rights -- it must not be allowed to become a wasteland.

Truth and justice for the Iraqi people was Sergio's goal. The principles that he held so dear in life must not be sacrificed now. The perpetrators must be apprehended and brought to justice but his death must not become a pretext for a witch hunt nor lead to widespread abuse of human rights -- no arbitrary arrests, no arbitrary detentions, no excessive use of force.

There are those who will see this tragedy as proof that Sergio was wrong in his approach to Iraq -- respect for human rights and participation of the Iraqi people.

But Amnesty International and other human rights activists know that only by putting human rights at the heart of security can this meaningless violence be brought to an end. This is what Sergio believed. This is what he and his colleagues worked and died for.

The killing of the UN High Commissioner for Human Rights is an outrageous attack on human rights defenders everywhere. We will not let it pass. Our grief only strengthens our resolve for action. They killed the man, they can never kill his legacy.

§ A UNIQUE COCKTAIL OF QUALITIES AND IDENTITIES

By Andreas Sandre von Warburg *

- In September 2007, the Secretary-General appointed
you as his Special Representative in Iraq, a post once held
by Sergio Vieira de Mello; a post that cost Sergio's life and
the lives of 22 members of his staff. What went through
your mind when the Secretary-General asked you to leave
the helm of the United Nations Staff College in Turin, Italy,
and head the UN Mission in Baghdad?

- Two thoughts came to mind. First, the United Nations had
a role to play in Iraq and we owed it to the Iraqis in what is
going to be probably the most crucial year in this period
of their current history. The UN had been in Iraq for the
past 30 years with a limited mandate. When the

---

* Interview with Staffan De Mistura, Special Representative of the UN Secretary-General in Iraq (February 15, 2008)

Organization has been asked through a new Security Council resolution to go back to Iraq with a stronger mandate, and the Secretary-General had the confidence in wanting me there to lead the mission, I felt I could not turn down the offer. It would have been like a medical doctor, after performing delicate and complicated surgeries for many years, all of the sudden, feeling a little bit more comfortable in a nice place like Torino, he refuses to treat an important but very complicated patient. That doctor – with his long experience with difficult cases – could have been one of the very few who could help. But instead he said "No, I want to open a health spa in Torino. Sorry! I'm not going to do the surgery." Well, like that doctor I felt I could not say "No" and betray the legacy of Sergio, the loyalty to his memory, and the dedication of the many UN staff members who operate on a daily basis in a very difficult and dangerous environment, putting their lives at risk.

My second thought when the Secretary-General asked me to lead the new UN mission in Baghdad, was Sergio's sacrifice. I feel, just like many colleagues at the United Nations who knew him – but even those who never met him – Sergio's death should not be in vain. Those who killed him should not feel that by doing so they stopped the UN for helping the Iraqis.

– According to New York Times journalist James Traub in his book "The Best Intentions: Kofi Annan and the UN in the Era of American World Power," Sergio Vieira de Mello had originally turned down the appointment before being *persuaded by the White House and then- US Secretary of State Condoleezza Rice. Do you think his first reaction was mostly due to the security situation in Iraq? Or rather, his decision to finally go was due to pressures from Turtle Bay? "Certainly Kofi Annan bitterly blamed himself for sending Sergio to his death," as former UN Under-Secretary-General for Communications and Public Information Shashi Tharoor recounts in a letter to the editor of the London Review of Books.*

– I knew Sergio quite well. We were good friends. We use to speak Italian, which he spoke extremely well having lived in Italy for a lmany years when his father was a diplomat there. We had a lot in common in terms of sharing experiences and being often in parallel missions – and I recall several of those. I know he had very similar reasons for which I accepted the Secretary-General appointment in Iraq. In fact, we discussed it. Sergio felt he could not turned down Kofi Annan's offer to lead the UN in what was anyway the crucial moment for the country in its post-conflict period. It was a difficult decision for him and his family.

The United Nations had a very limited mandate, but it was returning with the intention to try to make a difference. To help the Iraqis in rebuilding their country. Sergio felt it was the time to do so. At the same time, he felt – also due to personal reasons – that this mission was probably going to be shorter than previous ones he led. Sergio came from a three year mission as UN Administrator in East Timor and, shortly before going to Iraq, he was appointed UN High-

Commissioner for Human Rights In Geneva, a major challenge in his life and career. You don't leave that job, which is a mission in itself, without jeopardizing the impact that you can have, apart from personal reasons for not being too far and too long away – we all have a family, we all have personal reasons for not being away from our loved-ones in difficult situations. At the same time, Sergio did not want to jeopardize a mission that he had accepted and obtained, which for him was the promotion and the protection of Human Rights around the world.

You also have to understand that Iraq at the time was at all a danger, not as we perceive it now. Back then, Iraq was not as dangerous as now. Our international staff was living in town. They were circulating normally. They were eating at restaurants in Baghdad, shopping at the bazaar. They were not subjected to the attacks that became a pattern after the suicide bombing that killed him and his staff in 2003. In my opinion, I don't think security was in his considerations. After all, Sergio was a very courageous person, and extremely conscious about the dangers of its mission.

– "Knowing Sergio as I did for a quarter-century, I believe he was impelled by the sense of duty that had always characterized his willingness to take on hazardous and far-flung assignments, often at a moment's notice," Tharoor described the former UN envoy. How do you remember Sergio – as a colleague and as a friend?

– I remember Sergio as someone who had a unique

cocktail of qualities and identities. He was extremely sophisticated, refined. He was intellectually very attractive and even physically he was extremely pleasant. He was always smiling; certainly smiling in a disarming way. He was a mentor and a very good friend to many. It was difficult not to be friend with Sergio. At the same time, his unique charm was combined with a profound idealistic motivation for the very reasons he was doing that job. His vision for the United Nations grew through various steps of difficult assignments where you are confronted with harsh reality checks and you have grown a certain level of calm outrage towards injustices. He had a very strong determination to fight injustices, whatever they were: raging intestine wars, hunger, refugees, development, civil and human rights. That aspect was there, combined with quite a unique creativity to find solutions to complicated problems. With a touch of diplomacy and a touch of pragmatism, combined together with the charm he had to convey political messages, he was often making things happen. Last but not least, he was someone who was extremely well-dressed both externally and internally. He was extremely at ease in the most sophisticated capitals. And even when he was settling comfortably in a capital, he was missing the field. And that is where I agree with the Shashi Taroor's comment: he could not turn down a challenging mission; he was impelled by the sense of duty. Several times in my long friendship with Sergio I remember discussing challenges he was offered or eager to undertake in the field, leaving even very prestigious assignments at headquarters.

– Your mandate in Iraq is different from that of Sergio Vieira de Mello. The United Nations all but withdrew from Iraq in 2004, right after the suicide bombing attack at the UN Headquarters in Baghdad, and slowly started to re-established its presence only in mid 2007. You're the first new UN envoy since the Security Council passed Resolution 1770, allowing the newly-expanded mission to "advise, support and assist" the Iraqi Government in advancing an "inclusive, national dialogue and political reconciliation", reviewing the Constitution, setting internal boundaries, and dealing with the millions of Iraqis who have fled their homes. How would you describe the differences in your mandate and that of Sergio?

– Each period of each mission changes depending on the circumstances on the ground. The roles change. Iraq changed enormously from the time Sergio arrived in Baghdad. It was a completely different situation in terms of security and the level of tension among the various players, and in terms of the relationships with neighboring countries. We also have to consider the fact that the infiltration of Al-Qaida took place afterwards. Iraq was a different place, a different country.

Sergio had indeed a limited mandate from the United Nations Security Council, which made his mission very difficult. In this sense, the role he played was even more admirable, and to have an impact out of his very limited mandate was indeed an extraordinary achievement. Most of the decisions – good decisions – which took place during that period we know now were strongly influenced by Sergio's own lobbying and convincing work. Lets make it clear: the UN had no decision making power at the time; a largely different situation and experience compared to Sergio's role in East Timor, where he was in fact in charge of the interim administration.

The mission I've been assigned to is in a much more dangerous Iraq. The violence deteriorated substantially after the attack on Sergio in 2003. The UN left Iraq right after and came back full force only after resolution 1770 was passed by the Security Council. This is also a critical time for Iraq, where things seems to proceed better and with the UN backed by a strong resolution requesting the Organization to get involved actively to virtually any major issue relating to Iraq.

– *How's Sergio remembered in Iraq, by the Iraqis?*

– Everybody I meet here in Iraq asks me whether I knew him. And when I say he was a friend of mine and we worked together, they remember him with a lot of affection, respect, and sadness for his departure. In a sense, I'm grateful to Sergio and his work here in Iraq, because he made our mission easier. His legacy to our mission is reflected in our good relation with the Iraqis. They respect and abide someone who had represented the UN and worked for a better Iraq and a stronger UN.

– *What would be Sergio Vieira de Mello's legacy to the United Nations, to Iraq and to the World?*

– His legacy to the United Nations is that there is always a creative formula to move forward if: one, we are following are own mandate and our own mission and therefore there is no limit except our physical survival; two, having this combination of humanitarian and human rights expertise and political skills – which the UN gives the opportunity to develop during the years – is the formula to move effectively in complicated environments where the UN operates.

In other words, we need to become more like him: a cocktail of various experiences and various backgrounds in order to be as effective as we should. We should always be ready to go to the field and not stay – comfortably – at headquarters hoping things will improve. The combination of experiences on the field and at headquarters enriches the United Nations staff and the Organization, just like Sergio enriched it with his own constant search for a better world.

His legacy to the world shows that the UN has many weaknesses, many faults. But one of its great strength is people like Sergio. It's the UN own personnel around the world, the UN's own staff, the many people who are risking their lives for a better world, who are and have been dying for fulfilling the goals of the Organization. This is the strength of the United Nations and we need to foster it to make Sergio's sacrifice meaningful and not to betray his legacy.

– *You've been with the United Nations for well over 30*

years. You were posted to 19 war zones and negotiated very delicate deals. What would you suggest to those young people who are willing – like you and Sergio Vieira de Mello – to help the United Nations in its work around the world and pursue a career with the Organization?

I've been with the United Nations 37 years now, the exact numbers of years Sergio would have been with the Organization if he was still alive. My advice for all those young men and women who are thinking about joining the UN is to ask themselves if they are ready for the following: not to have a totally secure job – because the UN does not offer permanent contracts; to be ready to go to often difficult, complicated places, sometimes difficult to leave at a short notice; to move every two or three years and sometimes even more often; and to be facing moments of great frustration and disappointment for not being able to actually achieve what you were dreaming to achieve. If you have that and if you are open to multicultural, multilingual, multiethnic realities with a totally open heart, the other side of the coin is a unique a rewarding experience, combined with the feeling that, whatever you do, you are trying, even if you don't succeed, to do something useful to others – people that you have never met and may never meet. You are in a way involved in a politically – and physically – dangerous situation for a cause that has the power to mark history or the history of that village you are posted to. In spite of moments of frustration, you'll be experiencing incredible moments of joy when you see you'll be saving one or more lives with your work. And last but not least, you will have the privilege of learning so much from the very people you are trying to help, from their courage, their determination, their capacity of sustaining incredible situations, incredible pressures. If you are ready to all of this, this is one of the best jobs in the world.

NADIA YOUNES

Matthew Couper
Nadia Younes
2011
Pencil on paper
7" x 5" / 175mm x 135mm
www.mattcouper.com

Nadia Younes
33 years in the United Nations.

1946 ~ 2003. Egypt.

Matthew Cofa 2011

"*I want you to think of Nadia and all of the U.N. workers who are often forgotten. They are the watchers of peace, the salt of the earth.*"

— *Bernard Kouchner*
Co-founder of Médecins Sans Frontières

§ THE EGYPTIAN PRINCESS

By Andreas Sandre von Warburg

Nadia Younes was serving as Chief of Staff for Sergio Vieira de Mello, the United Nations Special Representative in Iraq, when in August 2003 – only a few months into her new appointment – a terrorist attack struck the UN headquarters in Bagdad. Both Nadia and Sergo lost their lives, alongside 15 other dedicated UN staff members.

Her posting to Bagdad was an important step in Nadia's career. One of her closest friends, Mona Makram Ebeid, professor of political science at the American University in Cairo and former member of parliament, remembered: "How ironical and cruelly sad that just a week before the vicious bombing (...), I was conversing with Iqbal Reza, Kofi Anan's chief of staff, who happened to be attending the Assila Conference with me in Morocco, when he announced that Nadia had just been promoted to become Assistant Secretary-General of the United Nations. It was a dream she had always nurtured; how cruel that it was in Baghdad that her career peaked and her life ended."

Indeed, Nadia's career embodied the values and spirit of the United Nations. She joined the UN Secretariat in New York in 1970 in the Office of General Services. From 1974 she worked with the Department of Public Information in various capacities, initially as a press officer in both the English and French Sections. Later assignments included Information Officer for the World Conference of the Decade for Women; Information Office, Planning, Programme and Evaluation Unit; and later Spokeswoman for the President of the Forty-Second Session of the General Assembly.

Nadia, an Egyptian national with a Master of Arts degree in political sciences and international relations from New York University, had her first big break in 1988, when she served as Deputy Spokesperson for the Secretary-General, a position she held until January 1993, serving under Javier Pérez de Cuéllar and later Boutros Boutros-Ghali.

After a stint in Rome, Italy, as Director of the United Nations Information Centre, she moved back to New York to assume the post of Director of the Media Division in the Department of Public Information. In 1998 she became Chief of Protocol of the United Nations.

In her role "she had a major role in organizing the millennium summit meeting, as well as the responsibility for keeping feathers unruffled during the three-day gathering," as Paul Lewis wrote in 2003 in the New York Times. "That the meeting, mainly devoted to brainstorming about the coming century, went off smoothly was in large measure attributed to Ms. Younes's dextrous handling of the assembled potentates."

Her key role as Chief of Protocol is very evident in the 2003 documentary movie Kofi Annan: Center of the Storm, which follows Secretary-General Annan, winner of the 2001 Nobel Peace Prize, during his trip to Stockholm, Sweden, to accept the award, and to East Timor, to celebrate the country's new independence. With unprecedented access given to the filmmakers and to director David Grubin, the documentary shows the daily life of the UN Head as well as of his immediate entourage, including a very strong Nadia. She, according to many, made that trip of Annan's most successful, thanks mostly to her dedication, political acumen, and straightforward attitude.

"Nadia was a chain-smoking, hard-drinking, hard-laughing person who wouldn't put up with pompous, bureaucratic people," wrote one of her best friends, Zohreh 'Zuzu' Tabatabai, in her eulogy. "She loved putting pins in the vain bureaucrats, the toadies. She would do it quite elegantly: put a pin in them and the air would go out of them and they would never know what hit them."

Tabatabai, most recently Director of Communications and Public Information at the UN International Labour Organization in Geneva, started working at the United Nations with Nadia. "We were like sisters," she wrote in an open letter. "To remember Nadia is to remember her laugh. She would throw her head back and laugh, with that husky voice. She was always laughing. She said 'You don't have to be serious just because something is important.' Whenever she walked into the room, there was electricity, everything became more fun. She always had these stories that made people laugh, and she would retell them, and each time they became more and more grand, and more and more funny. She never let the truth get in the way of a good story."

Her humor and laugh are remembered by all her friends and co-workers.

"It's hard to forget Nadia's good sense of humor, her loud laughter – you could hear her laughing from afar," remembers Peter Paulose, Nadia's deputy during her years as UN Chief of Protocol. "She could laugh louder than anybody else."

According to her friend Mona Ebeid, "what was refreshing about her was that she found humor in almost any stressful situation, whether it was Kosovo or Baghdad, shining like a bright star over long and stormy nights. 'My Egyptian princess' as she was called by Bernard Kouchner (then United Nations Administrator in Kosovo), whom she assisted in Kosovo."

Indeed, Kouchner, a former French Minister of Foreign Affairs and founder of Doctors Without Borders, knew her very well. She was in Kosovo as his spokesperson, from 1999 until 2001, while taking time off from her protocol duties. In Kosovo she learned a lot about working on the field, on very political issues. Following her assignment in Kosovo, Nadia returned to New York and resumed her functions as Chief of Protocol until August 2002, when she was appointed Executive Director of the World Health Organization in charge of External Relations under WHO Director General Gro Harlem Brundtland. Her position included responsibility for relations with Member States, resource mobilization, and governing bodies, the Executive Board and the World Health Assembly.

"She was very happy during that last year in Geneva," recalls Zohreh Tabatabai. "She had been working very hard in Kosovo and as Chief of Protocol in New York, and suddenly she came to this place which was the antithesis of Nadia. She started living in a different way, maybe it was a matter of maturity, but she liked going walking in the mountains."

§ A BURNING SENSE OF JUSTICE

By Kofi Annan [*]

It is wonderful to be here with you all at AUC. I am deeply honored to be invited to deliver this lecture in memory of my dear friend and colleague, Nadia Younes. How I wish she were still alive, and did not need to be commemorated.

As you know, Nadia was one of a group of the very best servants of the United Nations, whom we lost in one single, terrible blow on 19 August 2003. Another was Jean-Selim Kanaan, an outstanding Egyptian humanitarian, several of whose relatives are here with us today.

[*] Text of UN Secretary-General Kofi Annan's First Nadia Younes Memorial Lecture, delivered at the American University in Cairo (AUC), Egypt, on November 8, 2005. AUC established the Nadia Younes Memorial Fund in 2004. The fund supports a conference and meeting room on the new campus, an award for public and humanitarian service for graduating seniors and an annual lecture, all in Nadia Younes's name.

Jean-Selim was only 33 years old at the time of his death – which means he was born in the year that Nadia joined the United Nations. Had he lived, he would undoubtedly have had a career as distinguished as hers. Even in his short life, he had already rendered great service to the Organization, and to humanity, in several countries.

In her career, Nadia worked in New York, in Rome, in Kosovo, in Geneva, and last, of course, in Iraq. She contributed to many of the UN's successes, including the Beijing Women's Conference in 1995, the Millennium Summit in 2000 and the World Summit for Sustainable Development in 2002. She moved effortlessly from work in public information, where she served as spokeswoman for two of my predecessors, to being chief of protocol, and then to the World Health Organization, before being assigned to Baghdad as chief of staff to Sergio Vieira de Mello. And she was just about to come back to New York, as assistant secretary-general for General Assembly affairs, when her life was so cruelly cut short.

To all those places, and all those roles, she brought a burning sense of justice, leavened by extraordinary generosity of spirit and a wonderful sense of humour, as well as clear-eyed realism and excellent political antennae. Perhaps these qualities are best summed up in the words which her former colleagues have inscribed on the wall of the Spokesman's Office in New York: "She reached for the highest professional standards in her work, earned the respect and affection of her colleagues, and took profound pleasure in life. Her throaty laughter fills this room still."

Indeed, almost everyone who worked with her for more than a few weeks came to think of her as a special friend. I remember many solemn meetings that I could hardly have sat through, had not Nadia lightened them up by growling out some sardonic comment in that unforgettable gravelly voice. Without her, life at the UN has lost some of its savor.

Serving the UN inevitably takes you away from your home country – and so it took Nadia away from Egypt. She made the sacrifice of being away from her family and the friends of her youth, and from this city, which she loved so much.

But wherever she went, she brought with her something of this city, of this country and this region.

Her humor had a definite Cairene quality to it – the twinkle of an eye that has witnessed all the follies and foibles of humanity, and confronts them with infinite patience.

She was almost a prototype of the modern Egyptian woman. She wore the multiple identities implied in that phrase, together with the global identity that she effortlessly layered over them, with equal pride and equal comfort. For her, these various identities were never in conflict with each other.

And her moral stance was in the best traditions of the Arab intellectual. Her feeling of solidarity with Palestinian suffering, and her frustration at the prolonged occupation of Palestinian land, never stopped her from embracing Jews or Israelis as fellow human beings. Her anger, such as it was, was reserved for corrupt or oppressive rulers – in the Arab world and any where else in the world.

Her life began in Cairo and ended in Baghdad. She came as an Arab to work for the United Nations, and she returned to the Arab world bringing help from the United Nations to the suffering people of Iraq. She brought with her everywhere a special Arab brand of enlightenment and tolerance – only to fall victim, in the end, to a special brand of extremism and intolerance.

The lesson we must learn from her tragic death is that we need to work even harder to spread enlightenment and tolerance, and to overcome extremism and intolerance.

I'm sure we all remember what Iraq's situation was, in the summer of 2003. Opinions among Iraqis differed widely – as they still do – about the reasons for the foreign military presence in their country, about its consequences, and about the right way to respond.

It was foreseeable that some would choose to resist by force of arms. But what cannot be justified or accepted is the deliberate targeting of people who could in no way be identified with the foreign occupation: mainly Iraqi civilians, but also non-Iraqis like Nadia Younes and Jean-

Selim Kanaan who had come to Iraq without weapons, with the sole purpose of helping the Iraqi people. To target such people, or to throw a bomb inside a mosque or a school, is not resistance. It is murder. It is terrorism.

Nadia is not the only Arab diplomat to have fallen victim to such senseless, criminal violence in Iraq. It is right that I also pay homage here to the memory of Ihab al-Sherif, the Egyptian ambassador, and to the two Algerian diplomats, who were brutally murdered there earlier this year, and to countless other victims.

If anything can make such murders even worse, it is the fact that they appear to be part of a deliberate strategy to foster division and hatred, both within Iraq and in the wider world. The objective, it seems, is to turn Muslims not only against the west but against each other.

This tendency to divide humanity into mutually exclusive groups or categories, and to treat anyone who tries to cross the dividing lines as a traitor, is certainly not confined to the Middle East. It seems at times as if the whole world is falling prey to it.

We must break free from these cycles of violence and exclusion, which are stifling the human spirit. But we cannot do so by replying in kind. If we respond blindly to violence with violence, to anathema with anathema, to exclusion with exclusion, we will be accepting the logic of the very people we seek to defeat, and thereby helping them win new converts to their ideas.

On the contrary, we must respond to their logic with our own logic – the logic of peace, of reconciliation, of inclusion and mutual respect.

We must resolve, even more firmly, to build nations within which people of different communities can coexist, and enjoy equal rights.

We must resolve, as United Nations resolutions have repeatedly urged, to make the Middle East a region where all nations, including Israelis and Palestinians, can live side by side in peace and justice – each in their own state, within secure and recognized boundaries, free from threats or acts of force. In other words, we must keep alive the vision of a viable, contiguous Palestinian State.

And we must resolve to build a world in which no nation, and no community, will be punished collectively for the crimes of some of its members; a world in which no religion will be demonized for the aberrations of some of its adherents;; a world in which there will be no "clash of civilizations", because people will strive to discover the best in each other's traditions and cultures, and to learn from it. As I have said, the problem is not the faith but the faithful.

That is the kind of world that Nadia Younes stood for. It is the world that she worked for. It is the world which, in her own character, she pre-figured and personified. She was no starry-eyed utopian, but an idealist endowed with keen political insight and a clear understanding of the real world. At times, to a casual listener, she might even have sounded cynical. But a cynic does not risk her life to help bring about peace and progress in a land torn by conflict.

Nadia was a true daughter of Egypt, and no doubt Egypt could ill spare such an outstanding citizen. So we should be grateful to Egypt, not only for giving birth to her but also for seconding her, so to speak, to the cause of humanity – although of course in serving that cause she served Egypt's interest, too.

Too often, people speak as if there were a clash between national and global interests. But that is really a misconception. The global interest – the interest of humanity – includes, by definition, the interest of all nations. In the globalized and closely integrated world that we now inhabit, there are no longer any zero-sum games.

If we lose the battle against poverty, disease, injustice and environmental degradation, we will all lose.

If we allow conflict to persist between nations, or within them, we will all lose.

If we allow the continued proliferation of nuclear, radiological, chemical and biological weapons, we will all lose.

If we lose the battle against terrorism, we will all lose.

And if we fail to prevent or halt genocide, ethnic cleansing, war crimes and crimes against humanity, we will all lose – which is why I am greatly encouraged by the decision of world leaders, at the United Nations summit in September, to accept the responsibility to protect populations from such crimes, and their pledge to act in accordance with that responsibility.

But if we win the battle for justice – which means balanced and sustainable development, collective security, and universal human rights, underpinned by the rule of law both among nations and within them – then we will all win.

Those are not separate battles, but one – because, in the long run, we will not enjoy development without security, we will not enjoy security without development, and we will enjoy neither without respect for human rights.

To justice in that broad sense, comprising those three essential aspects of the UN's mission, Nadia Younes devoted, and in the end sacrificed, her life. The best way for us to commemorate her is to work even harder to achieve that goal.

§ SHE COULD LAUGH LOUDER THAN
  ANYBODY ELSE

By Andreas S. von Warburg [*]

– Nadia was part of your life as a UN official and as a friend. You had the privilege to experience her passion first hand and work under her guidance during her tenure at the Protocol Office. She was often described as a very passionate individual, with a strong character. How would you describe her, her personality, her work at the United Nations?

– It's hard to forget Nadia's good sense of humor, her loud laughter – you could hear her laughing from afar. She could laugh louder than anybody else. She was always a jolly good person, at work and in her private life. Even in the most difficult situations and tense environments, she

[*] Interview to Paulose Peter, former Deputy Chief of Protocol of the United Nations.

was able to loosen up and put anybody at ease. Nadia's humor came side-by-side with her biting sarcasm: Indeed, her good character and approachability were reflected in her work and work ethics. Nadia was undoubtedly born a leader: she was always in control of the situation and the harder the task, the better she performed. In control, but not a "control freak." Her part of her staff we had freedom of action. We could choose our own way to achieve results, as long as the job was done, and done well.

Nadia was very political savvy. She knew the United Nations extremely well and was able to put issues in their social, political, and economic context. She was probably not the most diplomatic person you would meet at the UN, but she knew the subject matter extremely well and mastered multilateral diplomacy as only few could. Her knowledge and experience made her a success story at the UN and I'm sure we would have seen much more form her.

– Is there any anecdote, memory you want to share?

– We were in Timor-Leste when it officially became an independent and sovereign nation. The United Nations were hosting the celebrations for the country's independence and dignitaries from around the world were traveling to Dili to attend the ceremonies. Since the UN was the host, we had to greet Heads of States and Government at the Airport. Both Nadia and I were there. A room was set up in order to receive high-level dignitaries. It was very nicely decorated: nice sofas, neatly furnished.

Right in the middle there was a small elegant coffee table and at the center, a very expensive urn, heavily decorated. A very nice antique. Nadia lighted a cigarette – she was a very heavy smoker. When she finished her cigarette, she didn't have any place to get rid of the cigarette butt. She looks around. The room was filled with people, many of them important VIPs. She said: "Where do I put it now?" And almost spontaneously, she went right for the urn. That's who she was. A very spontaneous and honest person; very forthright, very open, with no fuss.

– Nadia worked side-by-side former Secretary-General Kofi Annan for many years. As Chief of Protocol, she traveled throughout the world with the Secretary-General and had the opportunity to get to know him better probably than anyone else at the UN. What was the relationship between the two?

– This is a question that relates to the personal relationship between Kofi Annan and Nadia. From my perspective, it was clear she knew him very well. She had unfiltered and free access to him. My feeling is that anytime – day or night – she needed to talk to him, she could pick up the phone and speak directly to the Secretary-General. She called him Kofi, by his first name.

Nadia was also a good adviser to the then Secretary-General Annan. It is my understanding that he trusted her. In one occasion – she later confided –, Annan was trying to find a way to ease the increasing political tensions in a region. In a conversation with him, Nadia said: "Kofi, you pick up the phone and call this country (I am not naming the country here) and you tell this, this and this." He was very reluctant at first, but he followed Nadia's suggestion. That phone call helped tremendously and made the situation less tense. Eventually, he thanked her for such a spontaneous and honest advice. In other words, the relationship between the two – as far as I could see – was very open and honest, a reflection of Nadia's character and spirit of mind.

Because of this close relation with the Secretary-General, people – even colleagues – did not mess with her. They knew she was a close adviser to Mr. Annan. One time, during a large international conference away from the UN Headquarters, she brought the wrong head of State to a bilateral meeting with the Secretary-General who did not have even talking points with him because no such meeting was scheduled with that head of State. Though the Secretary-General knew that there was no such meeting scheduled, he gladly received him and had a meeting which went very well. Later, upon realizing the mistake, she went to the Secretary-General and apologized. Mr. Annan was not upset at all, and replied: "I know, don't worry Nadia."

– *More than anyone else, she knew exactly how to interact with a Secretary-General. In the early Nineties, she was Deputy Spokesperson for Javier Perez de Cuellar first, and Boutros-Boutros Ghali – an Egyptian like her – right after. Working so closely with the UN top management placed her in direct contact with the most disparate political and diplomatic issues of the time, as well as the large bureaucratic apparatus that often weighs on the UN. What were her feelings towards the United Nations? In other words, what did she like about the organization? Was there anything she wanted to change?*

– Nadia was a very loyal staff member. She strongly believed in the ideals of the United Nations. However, she hated all the bureaucracy that comes with it. Even as a Chief of Protocol, she was more interested in the issues debated at the UN than in the ceremonial aspects of the Organization. She couldn't stand the fuss and the beating-around-the-bush sort of attitude. Nadia had a more forthright get-to-the-point approach to her work.

– Being a woman in what many still call a "boy's club" must not have been easy. Do you think she ever felt discriminated against – as a woman, as a civilian peacekeeper? Was she a mentor for other women in her staff?

– I don't know if she felt discriminated against as a woman. She was a mentor, and not just for women. She was a mentor for her entire staff, regardless of gender, religion, or sexual orientation. She always gave credits to anybody who deserved it – women and men. If you were not doing your job properly, she would tell you right away... Maybe with a little humor and sarcasm, but she would definitely made you aware of your mistakes.

– Was she an inspiration, a mentor for you?

– She was. In many ways. In fact, Nadia was the one that promoted me to Assistant Chief of Protocol after the Millennium Summit. We all worked very hard in preparation to the Summit – one of the largest events organized on campus – and after all that hard work, she came to me and said: "I know you did very well. It's not in my hands to give you a promotion." She was able to upgrade my title. She laughingly said: "It does not come with financial implications, but it's something." She always showed her leadership and she always appreciated hard work. I always looked up to her, as a boss and as a friend. Indeed, she was a mentor in many ways.

– In his 2001 Nobel lecture, Annan said: "This award belongs not just to me. I do not stand here alone. On behalf of all my colleagues in every part of the United Nations, in every corner of the globe, who have devoted their lives – and in many instances risked or given their lives in the cause of peace – I thank the Members of the Nobel Committee for this high honour. My own path to service at the United Nations was made possible by the sacrifice and commitment of my family and many friends from all continents – some of whom have passed away – who taught me and guided me. To them, I offer my most profound gratitude." Nadia worked in very unstable regions: in Kosovo, with then UN Special Representative Bernard Kouchner, co-founder of Médecins Sans Frontières (Doctors Without Borders), and later in Iraq with Sergio Vieira de Mello. Had she ever thought about death and the risks associated with working in war zones? Had she *ever expressed fear?*

– Not that I know. She never looked for safe areas or comfortable zones where she could stay on and on. She never believed in being stagnant in one place, like a stick in the mud. She traveled the world with no fear. Even as a Chief of Protocol she could have find a comfortable spot, but she wanted a challenge. Whether in a war zone or back home at Headquarters, Nadia wanted to be challenged. As an international civil servant – a very effective one – she believed in moving forward. She had great ambitions. As you may know, she was supposed to come back to New York from Iraq as Assistant- Secretary-General and I'm sure that was not the last step of the ladder for her.

Nadia was not scared about going to areas where performing her job was difficult and challenging because of instability, war, or political tensions. Even if she was stationing in Iraq, she came back to New York several times to report on her work and the progression of the UN mission in the area. She never mentioned any fear. She was not scared. She was not in her character to be scared.

– She went to Iraq with great courage, devotion and commitment. In Baghdad, she lost her life, alongside Sergio Vieira de Mello and 12 other UN staff members. Do you think her death will contribute one day to a peaceful Iraq?

– Nadia and the other colleagues who lost their lives in

Baghdad made the ultimate sacrifice. Unfortunately, whether her sacrifice will contribute to a peaceful Iraq is still to be seen. But I do hope she didn't die in vain. As an international civil servant, she did was she had to do. And she did it extremely well. And even if, somehow selfishly, I want her to still be alive, there was no better way to put her convictions to the test and made the ultimate sacrifice for the cause. She would have done anything for the UN.

– What kind of legacy did she leave to us all?

– Strong belief in what you're doing, efficiency, responsibility, dedication, honesty, putting the United Nations and its ideals first without looking to a comfort zone and by conducting business as usual. These should be the hallmark of a true international civil servant. She is best remembered for all these qualities which were summed up and encapsulated in the personality of Nadia. She will be sorely missed by those who knew her.

ANNEXES

§ CHARTER OF THE UNITED NATIONS

Preamble

We the Peoples of the United Nations Determined

to save succeeding generations from the scourge of war, which twice in our lifetime has brought untold sorrow to mankind, and

to reaffirm faith in fundamental human rights, in the dignity and worth of the human person, in the equal rights of men and women and of nations large and small, and

to establish conditions under which justice and respect for the obligations arising from treaties and other sources of international law can be maintained, and to promote social progress and better standards of life in larger freedom,

And for these Ends

to practice tolerance and live together in peace with one another as good neighbors, and

to unite our strength to maintain international peace and security, and

to ensure by the acceptance of principles and the institution of methods, that armed force shall not be used, save in the common interest, and

to employ international machinery for the promotion of the economic and social advancement of all peoples,

Have Resolved to Combine our Efforts to Accomplish these Aims

Accordingly, our respective Governments, through representatives assembled in the city of San Francisco, who have exhibited their full powers found to be in good and due form, have agreed to the present Charter of the United Nations and do hereby establish an international organization to be known as the United Nations.

Chapter I

Purposes and Principles

Article 1

The Purposes of the United Nations are:

1. To maintain international peace and security, and to that end: to take effective collective measures for the prevention and removal of threats to the peace, and for the suppression of acts of aggression or other breaches of the peace, and to bring about by peaceful means, and in conformity with the principles of justice and international law, adjustment or settlement of international disputes or situations which might lead to a breach of the peace;

2. To develop friendly relations among nations based on respect for the principle of equal rights and self-determination of peoples, and to take other appropriate measures to strengthen universal peace;

3. To achieve international cooperation in solving international problems of an economic, social, cultural, or humanitarian character, and in promoting and encouraging respect for human rights and for fundamental freedoms for all without distinction as to race, sex, language, or religion; and

4. To be a center for harmonizing the actions of nations in the attainment of these common ends.

Article 2

The Organization and its Members, in pursuit of the Purposes stated in Article 1, shall act in accordance with the following Principles.

1. The Organization is based on the principle of the sovereign equality of all its Members.

2. All Members, in order to ensure to all of them the rights and benefits resulting from membership, shall fulfill in good faith the obligations assumed by them in accordance with the present Charter.

3. All Members shall settle their international disputes by peaceful means in such a manner that international peace and security, and justice, are not endangered.

4. All Members shall refrain in their international relations from the threat or use of force against the territorial integrity or political independence of any state, or in any other manner inconsistent with the Purposes of the United Nations.

5. All Members shall give the United Nations every assistance in any action it takes in accordance with the present Charter, and shall refrain from giving assistance to any state against which the United Nations is taking preventive or enforcement action.

6. The Organization shall ensure that states which are not Members of the United Nations act in accordance with these Principles so far as may be necessary for the maintenance of international peace and security.

7. Nothing contained in the present Charter shall authorize the United Nations to intervene in matters which are essentially within the domestic jurisdiction of any state or shall require the Members to submit such matters to settlement under the present Charter; but this principle shall not prejudice the application of enforcement measures under Chapter VII.

Chapter II
Membership

Article 3

The original Members of the United Nations shall be the states which, having participated in the United Nations Conference on International Organization at San Francisco, or having previously signed the Declaration by United Nations of January 1, 1942, sign the present Charter and ratify it in accordance with Article 110.

Article 4

1. Membership in the United Nations is open to all other peace-loving states which accept the obligations contained in the present Charter and, in the judgment of the Organization, are able and willing to carry out these obligations.

2. The admission of any such state to membership in the United Nations will be effected by a decision of the General Assembly upon the recommendation of the Security Council.

Article 5

A member of the United Nations against which preventive or enforcement action has been taken by the Security Council may be suspended from the exercise of the rights and privileges of membership by the General Assembly upon the recommendation of the Security Council. The exercise of these rights and privileges may be restored by the Security Council.

Article 6

A Member of the United Nations which has persistently violated the Principles contained in the present Charter may be expelled from the Organization by the General Assembly upon the recommendation of the Security Council.

Chapter III
Organs

Article 7

1. There are established as the principal organs of the United Nations: a General Assembly, a Security Council, an Economic and Social Council, a Trusteeship Council, an International Court of Justice, and a Secretariat.
2. Such subsidiary organs as may be found necessary may be established in accordance with the present Charter.

Article 8

The United Nations shall place no restrictions on the eligibility of men and women to participate in any capacity and under conditions of equality in its principal and subsidiary organs.

Chapter IV
The General Assembly

Composition

Article 9

1. The General Assembly shall consist of all the Members of the United Nations.

2. Each member shall have not more than five representatives in the General Assembly.

Functions and Powers

Article 10

The General Assembly may discuss any questions or any matters within the scope of the present Charter or relating to the powers and functions of any organs provided for in the present Charter, and, except as provided in Article 12, may make recommendations to the Members of the United Nations or to the Security Council or to both on any such questions or matters.

Article 11

1. The General Assembly may consider the general principles of cooperation in the maintenance of international peace and security, including the principles governing disarmament and the regulation of armaments, and may make recommendations with regard to such principles to the Members or to the Security Council or to both.

2. The General Assembly may discuss any questions relating to the maintenance of international peace and security brought before it by any Member of the United Nations, or by the Security Council, or by a state which is not a Member of the United Nations in accordance with Article 35, paragraph 2, and, except as provided in Article

12, may make recommendations with regard to any such questions to the state or states concerned or to the Security Council or to both. Any such question on which action is necessary shall be referred to the Security Council by the General Assembly either before or after discussion.

3. The General Assembly may call the attention of the Security Council to situations which are likely to endanger international peace and security.

4. The powers of the General Assembly set forth in this Article shall not limit the general scope of Article 10.

Article 12

1. While the Security Council is exercising in respect of any dispute or situation the functions assigned to it in the present Charter, the General Assembly shall not make any recommendation with regard to that dispute or situation unless the Security Council so requests.

2. The Secretary-General, with the consent of the Security Council, shall notify the General Assembly at each session of any matters relative to the maintenance of international peace and security which are being dealt with by the Security Council and shall similarly notify the General Assembly, or the Members of the United Nations if the General Assembly is not in session, immediately the Security Council ceases to deal with such matters.

Article 13

1. The General Assembly shall initiate studies and make recommendations for the purpose of:

a. promoting international cooperation in the political field and encouraging the progressive development of international law and its codification;

b. promoting international cooperation in the economic, social, cultural, educational, and health fields, and assisting in the realization of human rights and fundamental freedoms for all without distinction as to race, sex, language, or religion.

2. The further responsibilities, functions and powers of the General Assembly with respect to matters mentioned in paragraph 1(b) above are set forth in Chapters IX and X.

Article 14

Subject to the provisions of Article 12, the General Assembly may recommend measures for the peaceful adjustment of any situation, regardless of origin, which it deems likely to impair the general welfare or friendly relations among nations, including situations resulting from a violation of the provisions of the present Charter setting forth the Purposes and Principles of the United Nations.

Article 15

1. The General Assembly shall receive and consider annual and special reports from the Security Council; these reports shall include an account of the measures that the Security Council has decided upon or taken to maintain international peace and security.

2. The General Assembly shall receive and consider reports from the other organs of the United Nations.

Article 16

The General Assembly shall perform such functions with respect to the international trusteeship system as are assigned to it under Chapters XII and XIII, including the approval of the trusteeship agreements for areas not designated as strategic.

Article 17

1. The General Assembly shall consider and approve the budget of the Organization.

2. The expenses of the Organization shall be borne by the Members as apportioned by the General Assembly.

3. The General Assembly shall consider and approve any financial and budgetary arrangements with specialized agencies referred to in Article 57 and shall examine the administrative budgets of such specialized agencies with a view to making recommendations to the agencies concerned.

Voting

Article 18

1. Each member of the General Assembly shall have one vote.

2. Decisions of the General Assembly on important questions shall be made by a two-thirds majority of the members present and voting. These questions shall include: recommendations with respect to the maintenance of international peace and security, the election of the non-permanent members of the Security Council, the election of the members of the Economic

and Social Council, the election of members of the Trusteeship Council in accordance with paragraph 1(c) of Article 86, the admission of new Members to the United Nations, the suspension of the rights and privileges of membership, the expulsion of Members, questions relating to the operation of the trusteeship system, and budgetary questions.

3. Decisions on other questions, Composition including the determination of additional categories of questions to be decided by a two-thirds majority, shall be made by a majority of the members present and voting.

Article 19

A Member of the United Nations which is in arrears in the payment of its financial contributions to the Organization shall have no vote in the General Assembly if the amount of its arrears equals or exceeds the amount of the contributions due from it for the preceding two full years. The General Assembly may, nevertheless, permit such a Member to vote if it is satisfied that the failure to pay is due to conditions beyond the control of the Member.

Procedure

Article 20

The General Assembly shall meet in regular annual sessions and in such special sessions as occasion may require. Special sessions shall be convoked by the Secretary-General at the request of the Security Council or of a majority of the Members of the United Nations.

Article 21

The General Assembly shall adopt its own rules of procedure. It shall elect its President for each session.

Article 22

The General Assembly may establish such subsidiary organs as it deems necessary for the performance of its functions.

Chapter V
The Security Council

Article 23

1. The Security Council shall consist of fifteen Members of the United Nations. The Republic of China, France, the Union of Soviet Socialist Republics, the United Kingdom of Great Britain and Northern Ireland, and the United States of America shall be permanent members of the Security Council. The General Assembly shall elect ten other Members of the United Nations to be non-permanent members of the Security Council, due regard being specially paid, in the first instance to the contribution of Members of the United Nations to the maintenance of international peace and security and to the other purposes of the Organization, and also to equitable geographical distribution.

The non-permanent members of the Security Council shall be elected for a term of two years. In the first election of the non-permanent members after the increase of the membership of the Security Council from eleven to fifteen, two of the four additional members shall be chosen for a term of one year. A retiring member shall not be eligible for immediate re-election.

Each member of the Security Council shall have one representative.

Functions and Powers

Article 24

1. In order to ensure prompt and effective action by the United Nations, its Members confer on the Security Council primary responsibility for the maintenance of international peace and security, and agree that in carrying out its duties under this responsibility the Security Council acts on their behalf.

2. In discharging these duties the Security Council shall act in accordance with the Purposes and Principles of the United Nations. The specific powers granted to the Security Council for the discharge of these duties are laid down in Chapters VI, VII, VIII, and XII.

3. The Security Council shall submit annual and, when necessary, special reports to the General Assembly for its consideration.

Article 25

The Members of the United Nations agree to accept and carry out the decisions of the Security Council in accordance with the present Charter.

Article 26

In order to promote the establishment and maintenance of international peace and security with the least diversion for armaments of the world's human and economic resources, the Security Council shall be responsible for formulating, with the assistance of the Military Staff Committee referred to in Article 47, plans to be submitted to the Members of the United Nations for the establishment of a system for the regulation of armaments.

Voting

Article 27

1. Each member of the Security Council shall have one vote.

2. Decisions of the Security Council on procedural matters shall be made by an affirmative vote of nine members.

3. Decisions of the Security Council on all other matters shall be made by an affirmative vote of nine members including the concurring votes of the permanent members; provided that, in decisions under Chapter VI, and under paragraph 3 of Article 52, a party to a dispute shall abstain from voting.

Procedure

Article 28

1. The Security Council shall be so organized as to be able to function continuously. Each member of the Security Council shall for this purpose be represented at all times at the seat of the Organization.

2. The Security Council shall hold periodic meetings at which each of its members may, if it so desires, be

represented by a member of the government or by some other specially designated representative.

3. The Security Council may hold meetings at such places other than the seat of the Organization as in its judgment will best facilitate its work.

Article 29

The Security Council may establish such subsidiary organs as it deems necessary for the performance of its functions.

Article 30

The Security Council shall adopt its own rules of procedure, including the method of selecting its President.

Article 31

Any Member of the United Nations which is not a member of the Security Council may participate, without vote, in the discussion of any question brought before the Security Council whenever the latter considers that the interests of that Member are specially affected.

Article 32

Any Member of the United Nations which is not a member of the Security Council or any state which is not a Member of the United Nations, if it is a party to a dispute under consideration by the Security Council, shall be invited to participate, without vote, in the discussion relating to the dispute. The Security Council shall lay down such conditions as it deems just for the participation of a state which is not a Member of the United Nations.

Chapter VI

Pacific Settlement of Disputes

Article 33

1. The parties to any dispute, the continuance of which is likely to endanger the maintenance of international peace and security, shall, first of all, seek a solution by negotiation, enquiry, mediation, conciliation, arbitration, judicial settlement, resort to regional agencies or arrangements, or other peaceful means of their own choice.

2. The Security Council shall, when it deems necessary, call upon the parties to settle their dispute by such means.

Article 34

The Security Council may investigate any dispute, or any situation which might lead to international friction or give rise to a dispute, in order to determine whether the continuance of the dispute or situation is likely to endanger the maintenance of international peace and security.

Article 35

1. Any Member of the United Nations may bring any dispute, or any situation of the nature referred to in Article 34, to the attention of the Security Council or of the General Assembly.

2. A state which is not a Member of the United Nations may bring to the attention of the Security Council or of the General Assembly any dispute to which it is a party if it accepts in advance, for the purposes of the dispute, the

obligations of pacific settlement provided in the present Charter.

3. The proceedings of the General Assembly in respect of matters brought to its attention under this Article will be subject to the provisions of Articles 11 and 12.

Article 36

1. The Security Council may, at any stage of a dispute of the nature referred to in Article 33 or of a situation of like nature, recommend appropriate procedures or methods of adjustment.

2. The Security Council should take into consideration any procedures for the settlement of the dispute which have already been adopted by the parties.

3. In making recommendations under this Article the Security Council should also take into consideration that legal disputes should as a general rule be referred by the parties to the International Court of Justice in accordance with the provisions of the Statute of the Court.

Article 37

1. Should the parties to a dispute of the nature referred to in Article 33 fail to settle it by the means indicated in that Article, they shall refer it to the Security Council.

2. If the Security Council deems that the continuance of the dispute is in fact likely to endanger the maintenance of international peace and security, it shall decide whether to take action under Article 36 or to recommend such terms of settlement as it may consider appropriate.

Article 38

Without prejudice to the provisions of Articles 33 to 37, the Security Council may, if all the parties to any dispute so request, make recommendations to the parties with a view to a pacific settlement of the dispute.

Chapter VII
Action with respect to threats to the peace, breaches of the peace, and acts of aggression

Article 39

The Security Council shall determine the existence of any threat to the peace, breach of the peace, or act of aggression and shall make recommendations, or decide what measures shall be taken in accordance with Articles 41 and 42, to maintain or restore international peace and security.

Article 40

In order to prevent an aggravation of the situation, the Security Council may, before making the recommendations or deciding upon the measures provided for in Article 39, call upon the parties concerned to comply with such provisional measures as it deems necessary or desirable. Such provisional measures shall be without prejudice to the rights, claims, or position of the parties concerned. The Security Council shall duly take account of failure to comply with such provisional measures.

Article 41

The Security Council may decide what measures not involving the use of armed force are to be employed to give effect to its decisions, and it may call upon the Members of the United Nations to apply such measures. These may include complete or partial interruption of economic relations and of rail, sea, air, postal, telegraphic, radio, and other means of communication, and the severance of diplomatic relations.

Article 42

Should the Security Council consider that measures provided for in Article 41 would be inadequate or have proved to be inadequate, it may take such action by air, sea, or land forces as may be necessary to maintain or restore international peace and security. Such action may include demonstrations, blockade, and other operations by air, sea, or land forces of Members of the United Nations.

Article 43

1. All Members of the United Nations, in order to contribute to the maintenance of international peace and security, undertake to make available to the Security Council, on its call and in accordance with a special agreement or agreements, armed forces, assistance, and facilities, including rights of passage, necessary for the purpose of maintaining international peace and security.

2. Such agreement or agreements shall govern the numbers and types of forces. their degree of readiness

and general location, and the nature of the facilities and assistance to be provided.

3. The agreement or agreements shall be negotiated as soon as possible on the initiative of the Security Council. They shall be concluded between the Security Council and Members or between the Security Council and groups of Members and shall be subject to ratification by the signatory states in accordance with their respective constitutional processes.

Article 44

When the Security Council has decided to use force it shall, before calling upon a Member not represented on it to provide armed forces in fulfillment of the obligations assumed under Article 43, invite that Member, if the Member so desires, to participate in the decisions of the Security Council concerning the employment of contingents of that Member's armed forces.

Article 45

In order to enable the United Nations to take urgent military measures Members shall hold immediately available national air-force contingents for combined international enforcement action. The strength and degree of readiness of these contingents and plans for their combined action shall be determined, within the limits laid down in the special agreement or agreements referred to in Article 43, by the Security Council with the assistance of the Military Staff Committee.

Article 46

Plans for the application of armed force shall be made by the Security Council with the assistance of the Military Staff Committee.

Article 47

1. There shall be established a Military Staff Committee to advise and assist the Security Council on all questions relating to the Security Council's military requirements for the maintenance of international peace and security, the employment and command of forces placed at its disposal, the regulation of armaments, and possible disarmament.

2. The Military Staff Committee shall consist of the Chiefs of Staff of the permanent members of the Security Council or their representatives. Any Member of the United Nations not permanently represented on the Committee shall be invited by the Committee to be associated with it when the efficient discharge of the Committee's responsibilities requires the participation of that Member in its work.

3. The Military Staff Committee shall be responsible under the Security Council for the strategic direction of any armed forces placed at the disposal of the Security Council. Questions relating to the command of such forces shall be worked out subsequently.

4. The Military Staff Committee, with the authorization of the Security Council and after consultation with appropriate regional agencies, may establish regional subcommittees.

Article 48

1. The action required to carry out the decisions of the Security Council for the maintenance of international peace and security shall be taken by all the Members of the United Nations or by some of them, as the Security Council may determine.

2. Such decisions shall be carried out by the Members of the United Nations directly and through their action in the appropriate international agencies of which they are members.

Article 49

The Members of the United Nations shall join in affording mutual assistance in carrying out the measures decided upon by the Security Council.

Article 50

If preventive or enforcement measures against any state are taken by the Security Council, any other state, whether a Member of the United Nations or not, which finds itself confronted with special economic problems arising from the carrying out of those measures shall have the right to consult the Security Council with regard to a solution of those problems.

Article 51

Nothing in the present Charter shall impair the inherent right of individual or collective self-defense if an armed attack occurs against a Member of the United Nations, until the Security Council has taken measures necessary to maintain international peace and security. Measures taken by Members in the exercise of this right of self-defense shall be immediately reported to the Security Council and shall not in any way affect the authority and responsibility of the Security Council under the present Charter to take at any time such action as it deems necessary in order to maintain or restore international peace and security.

Chapter VIII
Regional arrangements

Article 52
1. Nothing in the present Charter precludes the existence of regional arrangements or agencies for dealing with such matters relating to the maintenance of international peace and security as are appropriate for regional action, provided that such arrangements or agencies and their activities are consistent with the Purposes and Principles of the United Nations.
2. The Members of the United Nations entering into such arrangements or constituting such agencies shall make every effort to achieve pacific settlement of local disputes through such regional arrangements or by such regional agencies before referring them to the Security Council.
3. The Security Council shall encourage the development of pacific settlement of local disputes through such regional arrangements or by such regional agencies either on the initiative of the states concerned or by reference from the Security Council.
4. This Article in no way impairs the application of Articles 34 and 35.

Article 53

1. The Security Council shall, where appropriate, utilize such regional arrangements or agencies for enforcement action under its authority. But no enforcement action shall be taken under regional arrangements or by regional agencies without the authorization of the Security Council, with the exception of measures against any enemy state, as defined in paragraph 2 of this Article, provided for pursuant to Article 107 or in regional arrangements directed against renewal of aggressive policy on the part of any such state, until such time as the Organization may, on request of the Governments concerned, be charged with the responsibility for preventing further aggression by such a state.

2. The term enemy state as used in paragraph 1 of this Article applies to any state which during the Second World War has been an enemy of any signatory of the present Charter.

Article 54

The Security Council shall at all times be kept fully informed of activities undertaken or in contemplation under regional arrangements or by regional agencies for the maintenance of international peace and security.

Chapter IX
International economic and social co-operation

Article 55

With a view to the creation of conditions of stability and well-being which are necessary for peaceful and friendly relations among nations based on respect for the principle of equal rights and self-determination of peoples, the United Nations shall promote:

a. higher standards of living, full employment, and conditions of economic and social progress and development;

b. solutions of international economic, social, health, and related problems; and international cultural and educational co-operation; and

c. universal respect for, and observance of, human rights and fundamental freedoms for all without distinction as to race, sex, language, or religion.

Article 56

All Members pledge themselves to take joint and separate action in cooperation with the Organization for the achievement of the purposes set forth in Article 55.

Article 57

1. The various specialized agencies, established by intergovernmental agreement and having wide international responsibilities, as defined in their basic instruments, in economic, social, cultural, educational, health, and related fields, shall be brought into relationship with the United Nations in accordance with the provisions of Article 63.

2. Such agencies thus brought into relationship with the United Nations are hereinafter referred to as specialized agencies.

Article 58
The Organization shall make recommendations for the coordination of the policies and activities of the specialized agencies.

Article 59
The Organization shall, where appropriate, initiate negotiations among the states concerned for the creation of any new specialized agencies required for the accomplishment of the purposes set forth in Article 55.

Article 60
Responsibility for the discharge of the functions of the Organization set forth in this Chapter shall be vested in the General Assembly and, under the authority of the General Assembly, in the Economic and Social Council, which shall have for this purpose the powers set forth in Chapter X.

Chapter X
The Economic and Social Council

Composition

Article 61
1. The Economic and Social Council shall consist of fifty-four Members of the United Nations elected by the General Assembly.

2. Subject to the provisions of paragraph 3, eighteen members of the Economic and Social Council shall be elected each year for a term of three years. A retiring member shall be eligible for immediate re-election.

3. At the first election after the increase in the membership of the Economic and Social Council from twenty-seven to fifty-four members, in addition to the members elected in place of the nine members whose term of office expires at the end of that year, twenty-seven additional members shall be elected. Of these twenty-seven additional members, the term of office of nine members so elected shall expire at the end of one year, and of nine other members at the end of two years, in accordance with arrangements made by the General Assembly.

4. Each member of the Economic and Social Council shall have one representative.

Functions and Powers

Article 62

1. The Economic and Social Council may make or initiate studies and reports with respect to international economic, social, cultural, educational, health, and related matters and may make recommendations with respect to any such matters to the General Assembly, to the Members of the United Nations, and to the specialized agencies concerned.

2. It may make recommendations for the purpose of promoting respect for, and observance of, human rights and fundamental freedoms for all.

3. It may prepare draft conventions for submission to the General Assembly, with respect to matters falling within its competence.

4. It may call, in accordance with the rules prescribed by the United Nations, international conferences on matters falling within its competence.

Article 63

1. The Economic and Social Council may enter into agreements with any of the agencies referred to in Article 57, defining the terms on which the agency concerned shall be brought into relationship with the United Nations. Such agreements shall be subject to approval by the General Assembly.

2. It may coordinate the activities of the specialized agencies through consultation with and recommendations to such agencies and through recommendations to the General Assembly and to the Members of the United Nations.

Article 64

1. The Economic and Social Council may take appropriate steps to obtain regular reports from the specialized agencies. It may make arrangements with the Members of the United Nations and with the specialized agencies to obtain reports on the steps taken to give effect to its own recommendations and to recommendations on matters falling within its competence made by the General Assembly.

2. It may communicate its observations on these reports to the General Assembly .

Article 65

The Economic and Social Council may furnish information to the Security Council and shall assist the Security Council upon its request.

Article 66

1. The Economic and Social Council shall perform such functions as fall within its competence in connection with the carrying out of the recommendations of the General Assembly.

2. It may, with the approval of the General Assembly, perform services at the request of Members of the United Nations and at the request of specialized agencies.

3. It shall perform such other functions as are specified elsewhere in the present Charter or as may be assigned to it by the General Assembly.

Article 67

1. Each member of the Economic and Social Council shall have one vote.

2. Decisions of the Economic and Social Council shall be made by a majority of the members present and voting.

Procedure

Article 68

The Economic and Social Council shall set up commissions in economic and social fields and for the promotion of human rights, and such other commissions as may be required for the performance of its functions.

Article 69

The Economic and Social Council shall invite any Member of the United Nations to participate, without vote, in its deliberations on any matter of particular concern to that Member.

Article 70

The Economic and Social Council may make arrangements for representatives of the specialized agencies to participate, without vote, in its deliberations and in those of the commissions established by it, and for its representatives to participate in the deliberations of the specialized agencies.

Article 71

The Economic and Social Council may make suitable arrangements for consultation with non-governmental organizations which are concerned with matters within its competence. Such arrangements may be made with international organizations and, where appropriate, with national organizations after consultation with the Member of the United Nations concerned.

Article 72

1. The Economic and Social Council shall adopt its own rules of procedure, including the method of selecting its President.

2. The Economic and Social Council shall meet as required in accordance with its rules, which shall include provision

for the convening of meetings on the request of a majority of its members.

Chapter XI
Declaration regarding non-self-governing territories

Article 73
Members of the United Nations which have or assume responsibilities for the administration of territories whose peoples have not yet attained a full measure of self-government recognize the principle that the interests of the inhabitants of these territories are paramount, and accept as a sacred trust the obligation to promote to the utmost, within the system of international peace and security established by the present Charter, the well-being of the inhabitants of these territories, and, to this end:
a. to ensure, with due respect for the culture of the peoples concerned, their political, economic, social, and educational advancement, their just treatment, and their protection against abuses;
b. to develop self-government, to take due account of the political aspirations of the peoples, and to assist them in the progressive development of their free political institutions, according to the particular circumstances of each territory and its peoples and their varying stages of advancement;
c. to further international peace and security;
d. to promote constructive measures of development, to encourage research, and to cooperate with one another and, when and where appropriate, with specialized international bodies with a view to the practical

achievement of the social, economic, and scientific purposes set forth in this Article; and

e. to transmit regularly to the Secretary-General for information purposes, subject to such limitation as security and constitutional considerations may require, statistical and other information of a technical nature relating to economic, social, and educational conditions in the territories for which they are respectively responsible other than those territories to which Chapter XII and XIII apply.

Article 74

Members of the United Nations also agree that their policy in respect of the territories to which this Chapter applies, no less than in respect of their metropolitan areas, must be based on the general principle of good-neighborliness, due account being taken of the interests and well-being of the rest of the world, in social, economic, and commercial matters.

Chapter XII
International trusteeship system

Article 75

The United Nations shall establish under its authority an international trusteeship system for the administration and supervision of such territories as may be placed thereunder by subsequent individual agreements. These territories are hereinafter referred to as trust territories.

Article 76

The basic objectives of the trusteeship system, in accordance with the Purposes of the United Nations laid down in Article 1 of the present Charter, shall be:

a. to further international peace and security;

b. to promote the political, economic, social, and educational advancement of the inhabitants of the trust territories, and their progressive development towards self-government or independence as may be appropriate to the particular circumstances of each territory and its peoples and the freely expressed wishes of the peoples concerned, and as may be provided by the terms of each trusteeship agreement;

c. to encourage respect for human rights and for fundamental freedoms for all without distinction as to race, sex, language, or religion, and to encourage recognition of the interdependence of the peoples of the world; and

d. to ensure equal treatment in social, economic, and commercial matters for all Members of the United Nations and their nationals and also equal treatment for the latter in the administration of justice without prejudice to the attainment of the foregoing objectives and subject to the provisions of Article 80.

Article 77

1. The trusteeship system shall apply to such territories in the following categories as may be placed thereunder by means of trusteeship agreements:

a. territories now held under mandate;

b. territories which may be detached from enemy states as a result of the Second World War, and

c. territories voluntarily placed under the system by states responsible for their administration.

2. It will be a matter for subsequent agreement as to which territories in the foregoing categories will be brought under the trusteeship system and upon what terms.

Article 78

The trusteeship system shall not apply to territories which have become Members of the United Nations, relationship among which shall be based on respect for the principle of sovereign equality.

Article 79

The terms of trusteeship for each territory to be placed under the trusteeship system, including any alteration or amendment, shall be agreed upon by the states directly concerned, including the mandatory power in the case of territories held under mandate by a Member of the United Nations, and shall be approved as provided for in Articles 83 and 85.

Article 80

1. Except as may be agreed upon in individual trusteeship agreements, made under Articles 77, 79, and 81, placing each territory under the trusteeship system, and until such agreements have been concluded, nothing in this Chapter shall be construed in or of itself to alter in any manner the rights whatsoever of any states or any peoples

or the terms of existing international instruments to which Members of the United Nations may respectively be parties.

2. Paragraph 1 of this Article shall not be interpreted as giving grounds for delay or postponement of the negotiation and conclusion of agreements for placing mandated and other territories under the trusteeship system as provided for in Article 77.

Article 81

The trusteeship agreement shall in each case include the terms under which the trust territory will be administered and designate the authority which will exercise the administration of the trust territory. Such authority, hereinafter called the administering authority, may be one or more states or the Organization itself.

Article 82

There may be designated, in any trusteeship agreement, a strategic area or areas which may include part or all of the trust territory to which the agreement applies, without prejudice to any special agreement or agreements made under Article 43.

Article 83

1. All functions of the United Nations relating to strategic areas, including the approval of the terms of the trusteeship agreements and of their alteration or amendment, shall be exercised by the Security Council.

2. The basic objectives set forth in Article 76 shall be applicable to the people of each strategic area.

3. The Security Council shall, subject to the provisions of the trusteeship agreements and without prejudice to security considerations, avail itself of the assistance of the Trusteeship Council to perform those functions of the United Nations under the trusteeship system relating to political. economic, social, and educational matters in the strategic areas.

Article 84
It shall be the duty of the administering authority to ensure that the trust territory shall play its part in the maintenance of international peace and security. To this end the administering authority may make use of volunteer forces, facilities, and assistance from the trust territory in carrying out the obligations towards the Security Council undertaken in this regard by the administering authority, as well as for local defense and the maintenance of law and order within the trust territory.

Article 85
1. The functions of the United Nations with regard to trusteeship agreements for all areas not designated as strategic, including the approval of the terms of the trusteeship agreements and of their alteration or amendment, shall be exercised by the General Assembly.
2. The Trusteeship Council, operating under the authority of the General Assembly, shall assist the General Assembly in carrying out these functions.

Chapter XIII
The Trusteeship Council

Composition

Article 86

1. The Trusteeship Council shall consist of the following Members of the United Nations:

a. those Members administering trust territories;

b. such of those Members mentioned by name in Article 23 as are not administering trust territories; and

c. as many other Members elected for three-year terms by the General Assembly as may be necessary to ensure that the total number of members of the Trusteeship Council is equally divided between those Members of the United Nations which administer trust territories and those which do not.

2. Each member of the Trusteeship Council shall designate one specially qualified person to represent it therein.

Functions and Powers

Article 87

The General Assembly and, under its authority, the Trusteeship Council, in carrying out their functions, may:

a. consider reports submitted by the administering authority;

b. accept petitions and examine them in consultation with the administering authority;

c. provide for periodic visits to the respective trust territories at times agreed upon with the administering authority; and

d. take these and other actions in conformity with the terms of the trusteeship agreements.

Article 88
The Trusteeship Council shall formulate a questionnaire on the political, economic, social, and educational advancement of the inhabitants of each trust territory, and the administering authority for each trust territory within the competence of the General Assembly shall make an annual report to the General Assembly upon the basis of such questionnaire.

Voting

Article 89
1. Each member of the Trusteeship Council shall have one vote.
2. Decisions of the Trusteeship Council shall be made by a majority of the members present and voting.

Procedure

Article 90
1. The Trusteeship Council shall adopt its own rules of procedure, including the method of selecting its President.
2. The Trusteeship Council shall meet as required in accordance with its rules, which shall include provision for the convening of meetings on the request of a majority of its members.

Article 91

The Trusteeship Council shall, when appropriate, avail itself of the assistance of the Economic and Social Council and of the specialized agencies in regard to matters with which they are respectively concerned.

Chapter XIV
The International Court of Justice

Article 92

The International Court of Justice shall be the principal judicial organ of the United Nations. It shall function in accordance with the annexed Statute which is based upon the Statute of the Permanent Court of International Justice and forms an integral part of the present Charter.

Article 93

1. All Members of the United Nations are ipso facto parties to the Statute of the International Court of Justice.

2. A state which is not a Member of the United Nations may become a party to the Statute of the International Court of Justice on conditions to be determined in each case by the General Assembly upon the recommendation of the Security Council.

Article 94

1. Each Member of the United Nations undertakes to comply with the decision of the International Court of Justice in any case to which it is a party.

2. If any party to a case fails to perform the obligations incumbent upon it under a judgment rendered by the

Court, the other party may have recourse to the Security Council, which may, if it deems necessary, make recommendations or decide upon measures to be taken to give effect to the judgment.

Article 95
Nothing in the present Charter shall prevent Members of the United Nations from entrusting the solution of their differences to other tribunals by virtue of agreements already in existence or which may be concluded in the future.

Article 96
1. The General Assembly or the Security Council may request the International Court of Justice to give an advisory opinion on any legal question.
2. Other organs of the United Nations and specialized agencies, which may at any time be so authorized by the General Assembly, may also request advisory opinions of the Court on legal questions arising within the scope of their activities.

Chapter XV
The Secretariat

Article 97
The Secretariat shall comprise a Secretary-General and such staff as the Organization may require. The Secretary-General shall be appointed by the General Assembly upon the recommendation of the Security Council. He

shall be the chief administrative officer of the Organization.

Article 98

The Secretary-General shall act in that capacity in all meetings of the General Assembly, of the Security Council, of the Economic and Social Council, and of the Trusteeship Council, and shall perform such other functions as are entrusted to him by these organs. The Secretary-General shall make an annual report to the General Assembly on the work of the Organization.

Article 99

The Secretary-General may bring to the attention of the Security Council any matter which in his opinion may threaten the maintenance of international peace and security.

Article 100

1. In the performance of their duties the Secretary-General and the staff shall not seek or receive instructions from any government or from any other authority external to the Organization. They shall refrain from any action which might reflect on their position as international officials responsible only to the Organization.

2. Each Member of the United Nations undertakes to respect the exclusively international character of the responsibilities of the Secretary-General and the staff and not to seek to influence them in the discharge of their responsibilities.

Article 101

1. The staff shall be appointed by the Secretary-General under regulations established by the General Assembly.

2. Appropriate staffs shall be permanently assigned to the Economic and Social Council, the Trusteeship Council, and, as required, to other organs of the United Nations. These staffs shall form a part of the Secretariat.

3. The paramount consideration in the employment of the staff and in the determination of the conditions of service shall be the necessity of securing the highest standards of efficiency, competence, and integrity. Due regard shall be paid to the importance of recruiting the staff on as wide a geographical basis as possible.

Chapter XVI
Miscellaneous provisions

Article 102

1. Every treaty and every international agreement entered into by any Member of the United Nations after the present Charter comes into force shall as soon as possible be registered with the Secretariat and published by it.

2. No party to any such treaty or international agreement which has not been registered in accordance with the provisions of paragraph I of this Article may invoke that treaty or agreement before any organ of the United Nations.

Article 103

In the event of a conflict between the obligations of the Members of the United Nations under the present Charter and their obligations under any other international agreement, their obligations under the present Charter shall prevail.

Article 104
The Organization shall enjoy in the territory of each of its Members such legal capacity as may be necessary for the exercise of its functions and the fulfillment of its purposes.

Article 105
1. The Organization shall enjoy in the territory of each of its Members such privileges and immunities as are necessary for the fulfillment of its purposes.
2. Representatives of the Members of the United Nations and officials of the Organization shall similarly enjoy such privileges and immunities as are necessary for the independent exercise of their functions in connection with the Organization.
3. The General Assembly may make recommendations with a view to determining the details of the application of paragraphs 1 and 2 of this Article or may propose conventions to the Members of the United Nations for this purpose.

Chapter XVII
Transitional security arrangements

Article 106
Pending the coming into force of such special agreements referred to in Article 43 as in the opinion of the Security Council enable it to begin the exercise of its responsibilities

under Article 42, the parties to the Four-Nation Declaration, signed at Moscow October 30, 1943, and France, shall, in accordance with the provisions of paragraph 5 of that Declaration, consult with one another and as occasion requires with other Members of the United Nations with a view to such joint action on behalf of the Organization as may be necessary for the purpose of maintaining international peace and security.

Article 107
Nothing in the present Charter shall invalidate or preclude action, in relation to any state which during the Second World War has been an enemy of any signatory to the present Charter, taken or authorized as a result of that war by the Governments having responsibility for such action.

Chapter XVIII
Amendments

Article 108
Amendments to the present Charter shall come into force for all Members of the United Nations when they have been adopted by a vote of two thirds of the members of the General Assembly and ratified in accordance with their respective constitutional processes by two thirds of the Members of the United Nations, including all the permanent members of the Security Council.

Article 109
1. A General Conference of the Members of the United Nations for the purpose of reviewing the present Charter

may be held at a date and place to be fixed by a two-thirds vote of the members of the General Assembly and by a vote of any seven members of the Security Council. Each Member of the United Nations shall have one vote in the conference.

2. Any alteration of the present Charter recommended by a two-thirds vote of the conference shall take effect when ratified in accordance with their respective constitutional processes by two thirds of the Members of the United Nations including all the permanent members of the Security Council.

3. If such a conference has not been held before the tenth annual session of the General Assembly following the coming into force of the present Charter, the proposal to call such a conference shall be placed on the agenda of that session of the General Assembly, and the conference shall be held if so decided by a majority vote of the members of the General Assembly and by a vote of any seven members of the Security Council.

Chapter XIX
Ratification and signature

Article 110
1. The present Charter shall be ratified by the signatory states in accordance with their respective constitutional processes.

2. The ratifications shall be deposited with the Government of the United States of America, which shall notify all the signatory states of each deposit as well as the Secretary-

General of the Organization when he has been appointed.

3. The present Charter shall come into force upon the deposit of ratifications by the Republic of China, France, the Union of Soviet Socialist Republics, the United Kingdom of Great Britain and Northern Ireland, and the United States of America, and by a majority of the other signatory states. A protocol of the ratifications deposited shall thereupon be drawn up by the Government of the United States of America which shall communicate copies thereof to all the signatory states.

4. The states signatory to the present Charter which ratify it after it has come into force will become original Members of the United Nations on the date of the deposit of their respective ratifications.

Article 111

The present Charter, of which the Chinese, French, Russian, English, and Spanish texts are equally authentic, shall remain deposited in the archives of the Government of the United States of America. Duly certified copies thereof shall be transmitted by that Government to the Governments of the other signatory states.

IN FAITH WHEREOF the representatives of the Governments of the United Nations have signed the present Charter.

DONE at the city of San Francisco the twenty-sixth day of June, one thousand nine hundred and forty-five.

§ UNIVERSAL DECLARATION
  OF HUMAN RIGHTS

Preamble

Whereas recognition of the inherent dignity and of the equal and inalienable rights of all members of the human family is the foundation of freedom, justice and peace in the world,

Whereas disregard and contempt for human rights have resulted in barbarous acts which have outraged the conscience of mankind, and the advent of a world in which human beings shall enjoy freedom of speech and belief and freedom from fear and want has been proclaimed as the highest aspiration of the common people,

Whereas it is essential, if man is not to be compelled to have recourse, as a last resort, to rebellion against tyranny and oppression, that human rights should be protected by the rule of law,

Whereas it is essential to promote the development of friendly relations between nations,

Whereas the peoples of the United Nations have in the Charter reaffirmed their faith in fundamental human rights, in the dignity and worth of the human person and in the equal rights of men and women and have determined to promote social progress and better standards of life in larger freedom,

Whereas Member States have pledged themselves to achieve, in co-operation with the United Nations, the promotion of universal respect for and observance of human rights and fundamental freedoms,

Whereas a common understanding of these rights and freedoms is of the greatest importance for the full realization of this pledge,

Now, Therefore THE GENERAL ASSEMBLY proclaims THIS UNIVERSAL DECLARATION OF HUMAN RIGHTS as a common standard of achievement for all peoples and all nations, to the end that every individual and every organ of society, keeping this Declaration constantly in mind, shall strive by teaching and education to promote respect for these rights and freedoms and by progressive measures, national and international, to secure their universal and effective recognition and observance, both among the peoples of Member States themselves and among the peoples of territories under their jurisdiction.

Article 1
All human beings are born free and equal in dignity and rights.They are endowed with reason and conscience and should act towards one another in a spirit of brotherhood.

Article 2
Everyone is entitled to all the rights and freedoms set forth in this Declaration, without distinction of any kind, such as race, colour, sex, language, religion, political or other opinion, national or social origin, property, birth or other status. Furthermore, no distinction shall be made on the basis of the political, jurisdictional or international status of the country or territory to which a person belongs, whether it be independent, trust, non-self-governing or under any other limitation of sovereignty.

Article 3
Everyone has the right to life, liberty and security of person.

Article 4
No one shall be held in slavery or servitude; slavery and the slave trade shall be prohibited in all their forms.

Article 5
No one shall be subjected to torture or to cruel, inhuman or degrading treatment or punishment.

Article 6

Everyone has the right to recognition everywhere as a person before the law.

Article 7

All are equal before the law and are entitled without any discrimination to equal protection of the law. All are entitled to equal protection against any discrimination in violation of this Declaration and against any incitement to such discrimination.

Article 8

Everyone has the right to an effective remedy by the competent national tribunals for acts violating the fundamental rights granted him by the constitution or by law.

Article 9

No one shall be subjected to arbitrary arrest, detention or exile.

Article 10

Everyone is entitled in full equality to a fair and public hearing by an independent and impartial tribunal, in the determination of his rights and obligations and of any criminal charge against him.

Article 11

(1) Everyone charged with a penal offence has the right to be presumed innocent until proved guilty according to

law in a public trial at which he has had all the guarantees necessary for his defence.

(2) No one shall be held guilty of any penal offence on account of any act or omission which did not constitute a penal offence, under national or international law, at the time when it was committed. Nor shall a heavier penalty be imposed than the one that was applicable at the time the penal offence was committed.

Article 12

No one shall be subjected to arbitrary interference with his privacy, family, home or correspondence, nor to attacks upon his honour and reputation. Everyone has the right to the protection of the law against such interference or attacks.

Article 13

(1) Everyone has the right to freedom of movement and residence within the borders of each state.

(2) Everyone has the right to leave any country, including his own, and to return to his country.

Article 14

(1) Everyone has the right to seek and to enjoy in other countries asylum from persecution.

(2) This right may not be invoked in the case of prosecutions genuinely arising from non-political crimes or from acts contrary to the purposes and principles of the United Nations.

Article 15

(1) Everyone has the right to a nationality.

(2) No one shall be arbitrarily deprived of his nationality nor denied the right to change his nationality.

Article 16

(1) Men and women of full age, without any limitation due to race, nationality or religion, have the right to marry and to found a family. They are entitled to equal rights as to marriage, during marriage and at its dissolution.

(2) Marriage shall be entered into only with the free and full consent of the intending spouses.

(3) The family is the natural and fundamental group unit of society and is entitled to protection by society and the State.

Article 17

(1) Everyone has the right to own property alone as well as in association with others.

(2) No one shall be arbitrarily deprived of his property.

Article 18

Everyone has the right to freedom of thought, conscience and religion; this right includes freedom to change his religion or belief, and freedom, either alone or in community with others and in public or private, to manifest his religion or belief in teaching, practice, worship and observance.

Article 19

Everyone has the right to freedom of opinion and expression; this right includes freedom to hold opinions without interference and to seek, receive and impart information and ideas through any media and regardless of frontiers.

Article 20

(1) Everyone has the right to freedom of peaceful assembly and association.

(2) No one may be compelled to belong to an association.

Article 21

(1) Everyone has the right to take part in the government of his country, directly or through freely chosen representatives.

(2) Everyone has the right of equal access to public service in his country.

(3) The will of the people shall be the basis of the authority of government; this will shall be expressed in periodic and genuine elections which shall be by universal and equal suffrage and shall be held by secret vote or by equivalent free voting procedures.

Article 22

Everyone, as a member of society, has the right to social security and is entitled to realization, through national effort and international co-operation and in accordance with the organization and resources of each State, of the economic, social and cultural rights indispensable for his dignity and the free development of his personality.

Article 23

(1) Everyone has the right to work, to free choice of employment, to just and favourable conditions of work and to protection against unemployment.

(2) Everyone, without any discrimination, has the right to equal pay for equal work.

(3) Everyone who works has the right to just and favourable remuneration ensuring for himself and his family an existence worthy of human dignity, and supplemented, if necessary, by other means of social protection.

(4) Everyone has the right to form and to join trade unions for the protection of his interests.

Article 24

Everyone has the right to rest and leisure, including reasonable limitation of working hours and periodic holidays with pay.

Article 25

(1) Everyone has the right to a standard of living adequate for the health and well-being of himself and of his family, including food, clothing, housing and medical care and necessary social services, and the right to security in the event of unemployment, sickness, disability, widowhood, old age or other lack of livelihood in circumstances beyond his control.

(2) Motherhood and childhood are entitled to special care and assistance. All children, whether born in or out of wedlock, shall enjoy the same social protection.

Article 26

(1) Everyone has the right to education. Education shall be free, at least in the elementary and fundamental stages. Elementary education shall be compulsory. Technical and professional education shall be made generally available and higher education shall be equally accessible to all on the basis of merit.

(2) Education shall be directed to the full development of the human personality and to the strengthening of respect for human rights and fundamental freedoms. It shall promote understanding, tolerance and friendship among all nations, racial or religious groups, and shall further the activities of the United Nations for the maintenance of peace.

(3) Parents have a prior right to choose the kind of education that shall be given to their children.

Article 27

(1) Everyone has the right freely to participate in the cultural life of the community, to enjoy the arts and to share in scientific advancement and its benefits.

(2) Everyone has the right to the protection of the moral and material interests resulting from any scientific, literary or artistic production of which he is the author.

Article 28

Everyone is entitled to a social and international order in which the rights and freedoms set forth in this Declaration can be fully realized.

Article 29

(1) Everyone has duties to the community in which alone the free and full development of his personality is possible.

(2) In the exercise of his rights and freedoms, everyone shall be subject only to such limitations as are determined by law solely for the purpose of securing due recognition and respect for the rights and freedoms of others and of meeting the just requirements of morality, public order and the general welfare in a democratic society.

(3) These rights and freedoms may in no case be exercised contrary to the purposes and principles of the United Nations.

Article 30

Nothing in this Declaration may be interpreted as implying for any State, group or person any right to engage in any activity or to perform any act aimed at the destruction of any of the rights and freedoms set forth herein.

§ CONVENTION ON THE ELIMINATION
  OF ALL FORMS OF DISCRIMINATION
  AGAINST WOMEN

The States Parties to the present Convention,

Noting that the Charter of the United Nations reaffirms faith in fundamental human rights, in the dignity and worth of the human person and in the equal rights of men and women,

Noting that the Universal Declaration of Human Rights affirms the principle of the inadmissibility of discrimination and proclaims that all human beings are born free and equal in dignity and rights and that everyone is entitled to all the rights and freedoms set forth therein, without distinction of any kind, including distinction based on sex,

Noting that the States Parties to the International Covenants on Human Rights have the obligation to ensure the equal rights of men and women to enjoy all economic, social, cultural, civil and political rights,

Considering the international conventions concluded under the auspices of the United Nations and the specialized agencies promoting equality of rights of men and women,

Noting also the resolutions, declarations and recommendations adopted by the United Nations and the specialized agencies promoting equality of rights of men and women,

Concerned, however, that despite these various instruments extensive discrimination against women continues to exist,

Recalling that discrimination against women violates the principles of equality of rights and respect for human dignity, is an obstacle to the participation of women, on equal terms with men, in the political, social, economic and cultural life of their countries, hampers the growth of the prosperity of society and the family and makes more difficult the full development of the potentialities of women in the service of their countries and of humanity,

Concerned that in situations of poverty women have the least access to food, health, education, training and opportunities for employment and other needs,

Convinced that the establishment of the new international economic order based on equity and justice will contribute significantly towards the promotion of equality between men and women,

Emphasizing that the eradication of apartheid, all forms of racism, racial discrimination, colonialism, neo-colonialism, aggression, foreign occupation and domination and interference in the internal affairs of States is essential to the full enjoyment of the rights of men and women,

Affirming that the strengthening of international peace and security, the relaxation of international tension, mutual co-operation among all States irrespective of their social and economic systems, general and complete disarmament, in particular nuclear disarmament under strict and effective international control, the affirmation of the principles of justice, equality and mutual benefit in relations among countries and the realization of the right of peoples under alien and colonial domination and foreign occupation to self-determination and independence, as well as respect for national sovereignty and territorial integrity, will promote social progress and development and as a consequence will contribute to the attainment of full equality between men and women,

Convinced that the full and complete development of a country, the welfare of the world and the cause of peace require the maximum participation of women on equal terms with men in all fields,

Bearing in mind the great contribution of women to the welfare of the family and to the development of society, so far not fully recognized, the social significance of maternity and the role of both parents in the family and in the upbringing of children, and aware that the role of women in procreation should not be a basis for discrimination but that the upbringing of children requires a sharing of responsibility between men and women and society as a whole,

Aware that a change in the traditional role of men as well as the role of women in society and in the family is needed to achieve full equality between men and women,

Determined to implement the principles set forth in the Declaration on the Elimination of Discrimination against Women and, for that purpose, to adopt the measures required for the elimination of such discrimination in all its forms and manifestations,

Have agreed on the following:

PART I

Article I

For the purposes of the present Convention, the term "discrimination against women" shall mean any distinction, exclusion or restriction made on the basis of sex which has the effect or purpose of impairing or nullifying the recognition, enjoyment or exercise by women, irrespective of their marital status, on a basis of equality of men and women, of human rights and fundamental freedoms in the political, economic, social, cultural, civil or any other field.

Article 2

States Parties condemn discrimination against women in all its forms, agree to pursue by all appropriate means and without delay a policy of eliminating discrimination against women and, to this end, undertake:

(a) To embody the principle of the equality of men and women in their national constitutions or other appropriate legislation if not yet incorporated therein and to ensure, through law and other appropriate means, the practical realization of this principle;

(b) To adopt appropriate legislative and other measures, including sanctions where appropriate, prohibiting all discrimination against women;

(c) To establish legal protection of the rights of women on an equal basis with men and to ensure through competent national tribunals and other public institutions the effective protection of women against any act of discrimination;

(d) To refrain from engaging in any act or practice of discrimination against women and to ensure that public authorities and institutions shall act in conformity with this obligation;

(e) To take all appropriate measures to eliminate discrimination against women by any person, organization or enterprise;

(f) To take all appropriate measures, including legislation, to modify or abolish existing laws, regulations, customs and practices which constitute discrimination against women;

(g) To repeal all national penal provisions which constitute discrimination against women.

Article 3

States Parties shall take in all fields, in particular in the political, social, economic and cultural fields, all appropriate measures, including legislation, to en sure the full development and advancement of women , for the purpose of guaranteeing them the exercise and enjoyment of human rights and fundamental freedoms on a basis of equality with men.

Article 4

1. Adoption by States Parties of temporary special measures aimed at accelerating de facto equality between men and women shall not be considered discrimination as defined in the present Convention, but shall in no way entail as a consequence the maintenance of unequal or separate standards; these measures shall be discontinued when the objectives of equality of opportunity and treatment have been achieved.

2. Adoption by States Parties of special measures, including those measures contained in the present Convention, aimed at protecting maternity shall not be considered discriminatory.

Article 5

States Parties shall take all appropriate measures:

(a) To modify the social and cultural patterns of conduct of men and women, with a view to achieving the elimination of prejudices and customary and all other practices which are based on the idea of the inferiority or the superiority of either of the sexes or on stereotyped roles for men and women;

(b) To ensure that family education includes a proper understanding of maternity as a social function and the recognition of the common responsibility of men and women in the upbringing and development of their children, it being understood that the interest of the children is the primordial consideration in all cases.

Article 6

States Parties shall take all appropriate measures, including legislation, to suppress all forms of traffic in women and exploitation of prostitution of women.

PART II

Article 7

States Parties shall take all appropriate measures to eliminate discrimination against women in the political and public life of the country and, in particular, shall ensure to women, on equal terms with men, the right:

(a) To vote in all elections and public referenda and to be eligible for election to all publicly elected bodies;

(b) To participate in the formulation of government policy and the implementation thereof and to hold public office and perform all public functions at all levels of government;

(c) To participate in non-governmental organizations and associations concerned with the public and political life of the country.

Article 8
States Parties shall take all appropriate measures to ensure to women, on equal terms with men and without any discrimination, the opportunity to represent their Governments at the international level and to participate in the work of international organizations.

Article 9
1. States Parties shall grant women equal rights with men to acquire, change or retain their nationality. They shall ensure in particular that neither marriage to an alien nor change of nationality by the husband during marriage shall automatically change the nationality of the wife, render her stateless or force upon her the nationality of the husband.
2. States Parties shall grant women equal rights with men with respect to the nationality of their children.

PART III

Article 10
States Parties shall take all appropriate measures to eliminate discrimination against women in order to ensure to them equal rights with men in the field of education and in particular to ensure, on a basis of equality of men and women:

(a) The same conditions for career and vocational guidance, for access to studies and for the achievement of diplomas in educational establishments of all categories in rural as well as in urban areas; this equality shall be ensured in pre-school, general, technical, professional and higher technical education, as well as in all types of vocational training;

(b) Access to the same curricula, the same examinations, teaching staff with qualifications of the same standard and school premises and equipment of the same quality;

(c) The elimination of any stereotyped concept of the roles of men and women at all levels and in all forms of education by encouraging coeducation and other types of education which will help to achieve this aim and, in particular, by the revision of textbooks and school programmes and the adaptation of teaching methods;

(d) The same opportunities to benefit from scholarships and other study grants;

(e) The same opportunities for access to programmes of continuing education, including adult and functional literacy programmes, particulary those aimed at reducing, at the earliest possible time, any gap in education existing between men and women;

(f) The reduction of female student drop-out rates and the organization of programmes for girls and women who have left school prematurely;

(g) The same Opportunities to participate actively in sports and physical education;

(h) Access to specific educational information to help to ensure the health and well-being of families, including information and advice on family planning.

Article 11

1. States Parties shall take all appropriate measures to eliminate discrimination against women in the field of employment in order to ensure, on a basis of equality of men and women, the same rights, in particular:

(a) The right to work as an inalienable right of all human beings;

(b) The right to the same employment opportunities, including the application of the same criteria for selection in matters of employment;

(c) The right to free choice of profession and employment, the right to promotion, job security and all benefits and conditions of service and the right to receive vocational training and retraining, including apprenticeships, advanced vocational training and recurrent training;

(d) The right to equal remuneration, including benefits, and to equal treatment in respect of work of equal value, as well as equality of treatment in the evaluation of the quality of work;

(e) The right to social security, particularly in cases of retirement, unemployment, sickness, invalidity and old age and other incapacity to work, as well as the right to paid leave;

(f) The right to protection of health and to safety in working conditions, including the safeguarding of the function of reproduction.

2. In order to prevent discrimination against women on the grounds of marriage or maternity and to ensure their effective right to work, States Parties shall take appropriate measures:

(a) To prohibit, subject to the imposition of sanctions, dismissal on the grounds of pregnancy or of maternity leave and discrimination in dismissals on the basis of marital status;

(b) To introduce maternity leave with pay or with comparable social benefits without loss of former employment, seniority or social allowances;

(c) To encourage the provision of the necessary supporting social services to enable parents to combine family obligations with work responsibilities and participation in public life, in particular through promoting the establishment and development of a network of child-care facilities;

(d) To provide special protection to women during pregnancy in types of work proved to be harmful to them.

3. Protective legislation relating to matters covered in this article shall be reviewed periodically in the light of scientific and technological knowledge and shall be revised, repealed or extended as necessary.

Article 12

1. States Parties shall take all appropriate measures to eliminate discrimination against women in the field of health care in order to ensure, on a basis of equality of men and women, access to health care services, including those related to family planning.

2. Notwithstanding the provisions of paragraph l of this article, States Parties shall ensure to women appropriate services in connection with pregnancy, confinement and the post-natal period, granting free services where

necessary, as well as adequate nutrition during pregnancy and lactation.

Article 13
States Parties shall take all appropriate measures to eliminate discrimination against women in other areas of economic and social life in order to ensure, on a basis of equality of men and women, the same rights, in particular:
(a) The right to family benefits;
(b) The right to bank loans, mortgages and other forms of financial credit;
(c) The right to participate in recreational activities, sports and all aspects of cultural life.

Article 14
1. States Parties shall take into account the particular problems faced by rural women and the significant roles which rural women play in the economic survival of their families, including their work in the non-monetized sectors of the economy, and shall take all appropriate measures to ensure the application of the provisions of the present Convention to women in rural areas.
2. States Parties shall take all appropriate measures to eliminate discrimination against women in rural areas in order to ensure, on a basis of equality of men and women, that they participate in and benefit from rural development and, in particular, shall ensure to such women the right:
(a) To participate in the elaboration and implementation of development planning at all levels;

(b) To have access to adequate health care facilities, including information, counselling and services in family planning;

(c) To benefit directly from social security programmes;

(d) To obtain all types of training and education, formal and non-formal, including that relating to functional literacy, as well as, inter alia, the benefit of all community and extension services, in order to increase their technical proficiency;

(e) To organize self-help groups and co-operatives in order to obtain equal access to economic opportunities through employment or self employment;

(f) To participate in all community activities;

(g) To have access to agricultural credit and loans, marketing facilities, appropriate technology and equal treatment in land and agrarian reform as well as in land resettlement schemes;

(h) To enjoy adequate living conditions, particularly in relation to housing, sanitation, electricity and water supply, transport and communications.

PART IV

Article 15

1. States Parties shall accord to women equality with men before the law.

2. States Parties shall accord to women, in civil matters, a legal capacity identical to that of men and the same opportunities to exercise that capacity. In particular, they shall give women equal rights to conclude contracts and

to administer property and shall treat them equally in all stages of procedure in courts and tribunals.

3. States Parties agree that all contracts and all other private instruments of any kind with a legal effect which is directed at restricting the legal capacity of women shall be deemed null and void.

4. States Parties shall accord to men and women the same rights with regard to the law relating to the movement of persons and the freedom to choose their residence and domicile.

Article 16

1. States Parties shall take all appropriate measures to eliminate discrimination against women in all matters relating to marriage and family relations and in particular shall ensure, on a basis of equality of men and women:

(a) The same right to enter into marriage;

(b) The same right freely to choose a spouse and to enter into marriage only with their free and full consent;

(c) The same rights and responsibilities during marriage and at its dissolution;

(d) The same rights and responsibilities as parents, irrespective of their marital status, in matters relating to their children; in all cases the interests of the children shall be paramount;

(e) The same rights to decide freely and responsibly on the number and spacing of their children and to have access to the information, education and means to enable them to exercise these rights;

(f) The same rights and responsibilities with regard to guardianship, wardship, trusteeship and adoption of children, or similar institutions where these concepts exist in national legislation; in all cases the interests of the children shall be paramount;

(g) The same personal rights as husband and wife, including the right to choose a family name, a profession and an occupation;

(h) The same rights for both spouses in respect of the ownership, acquisition, management, administration, enjoyment and disposition of property, whether free of charge or for a valuable consideration.

2. The betrothal and the marriage of a child shall have no legal effect, and all necessary action, including legislation, shall be taken to specify a minimum age for marriage and to make the registration of marriages in an official registry compulsory.

PART V

Article 17

1. For the purpose of considering the progress made in the implementation of the present Convention, there shall be established a Committee on the Elimination of Discrimination against Women (hereinafter referred to as the Committee) consisting, at the time of entry into force of the Convention, of eighteen and, after ratification of or accession to the Convention by the thirty-fifth State Party, of twenty-three experts of high moral standing and competence in the field covered by the Convention. The experts shall be elected by States Parties from among their nationals and shall serve in their personal capacity, consideration being given to equitable geographical

distribution and to the representation of the different forms of civilization as well as the principal legal systems.

2. The members of the Committee shall be elected by secret ballot from a list of persons nominated by States Parties. Each State Party may nominate one person from among its own nationals.

3. The initial election shall be held six months after the date of the entry into force of the present Convention. At least three months before the date of each election the Secretary-General of the United Nations shall address a letter to the States Parties inviting them to submit their nominations within two months. The Secretary-General shall prepare a list in alphabetical order of all persons thus nominated, indicating the States Parties which have nominated them, and shall submit it to the States Parties.

4. Elections of the members of the Committee shall be held at a meeting of States Parties convened by the Secretary-General at United Nations Headquarters. At that meeting, for which two thirds of the States Parties shall constitute a quorum, the persons elected to the Committee shall be those nominees who obtain the largest number of votes and an absolute majority of the votes of the representatives of States Parties present and voting.

5. The members of the Committee shall be elected for a term of four years. However, the terms of nine of the members elected at the first election shall expire at the end of two years; immediately after the first election the names of these nine members shall be chosen by lot by the Chairman of the Committee.

6. The election of the five additional members of the Committee shall be held in accordance with the provisions of paragraphs 2, 3 and 4 of this article, following the thirty-fifth ratification or accession. The terms of two of the additional members elected on this occasion shall expire at the end of two years, the names of these two members having been chosen by lot by the Chairman of the Committee.

7. For the filling of casual vacancies, the State Party whose expert has ceased to function as a member of the Committee shall appoint another expert from among its nationals, subject to the approval of the Committee.

8. The members of the Committee shall, with the approval of the General Assembly, receive emoluments from United Nations resources on such terms and conditions as the Assembly may decide, having regard to the importance of the Committee's responsibilities.

9. The Secretary-General of the United Nations shall provide the necessary staff and facilities for the effective performance of the functions of the Committee under the present Convention.

Article 18

1. States Parties undertake to submit to the Secretary-General of the United Nations, for consideration by the Committee, a report on the legislative, judicial, administrative or other measures which they have adopted to give effect to the provisions of the present Convention and on the progress made in this respect:

(a) Within one year after the entry into force for the State concerned;

(b) Thereafter at least every four years and further whenever the Committee so requests.

2. Reports may indicate factors and difficulties affecting the degree of fulfilment of obligations under the present Convention.

Article 19

1. The Committee shall adopt its own rules of procedure.

2. The Committee shall elect its officers for a term of two years.

Article 20

1. The Committee shall normally meet for a period of not more than two weeks annually in order to consider the reports submitted in accordance with article 18 of the present Convention.

2. The meetings of the Committee shall normally be held at United Nations Headquarters or at any other convenient place as determined by the Committee.

Article 21

1. The Committee shall, through the Economic and Social Council, report annually to the General Assembly of the United Nations on its activities and may make suggestions and general recommendations based on the examination of reports and information received from the States Parties. Such suggestions and general recommendations shall be included in the report of the Committee together with comments, if any, from States Parties.

2. The Secretary-General of the United Nations shall transmit the reports of the Committee to the Commission on the Status of Women for its information.

Article 22
The specialized agencies shall be entitled to be represented at the consideration of the implementation of such provisions of the present Convention as fall within the scope of their activities. The Committee may invite the specialized agencies to submit reports on the implementation of the Convention in areas falling within the scope of their activities.

PART VI

Article 23
Nothing in the present Convention shall affect any provisions that are more conducive to the achievement of equality between men and women which may be contained:
(a) In the legislation of a State Party; or
(b) In any other international convention, treaty or agreement in force for that State.

Article 24
States Parties undertake to adopt all necessary measures at the national level aimed at achieving the full realization of the rights recognized in the present Convention.

Article 25

1. The present Convention shall be open for signature by all States.

2. The Secretary-General of the United Nations is designated as the depositary of the present Convention.

3. The present Convention is subject to ratification. Instruments of ratification shall be deposited with the Secretary-General of the United Nations.

4. The present Convention shall be open to accession by all States. Accession shall be effected by the deposit of an instrument of accession with the Secretary-General of the United Nations.

Article 26

1. A request for the revision of the present Convention may be made at any time by any State Party by means of a notification in writing addressed to the Secretary-General of the United Nations.

2. The General Assembly of the United Nations shall decide upon the steps, if any, to be taken in respect of such a request.

Article 27

1. The present Convention shall enter into force on the thirtieth day after the date of deposit with the Secretary-General of the United Nations of the twentieth instrument of ratification or accession.

2. For each State ratifying the present Convention or acceding to it after the deposit of the twentieth instrument of ratification or accession, the Convention shall enter into force on the thirtieth day after the date of

the deposit of its own instrument of ratification or accession.

Article 28

1. The Secretary-General of the United Nations shall receive and circulate to all States the text of reservations made by States at the time of ratification or accession.

2. A reservation incompatible with the object and purpose of the present Convention shall not be permitted.

3. Reservations may be withdrawn at any time by notification to this effect addressed to the Secretary-General of the United Nations, who shall then inform all States thereof. Such notification shall take effect on the date on which it is received.

Article 29

1. Any dispute between two or more States Parties concerning the interpretation or application of the present Convention which is not settled by negotiation shall, at the request of one of them, be submitted to arbitration. If within six months from the date of the request for arbitration the parties are unable to agree on the organization of the arbitration, any one of those parties may refer the dispute to the International Court of Justice by request in conformity with the Statute of the Court.

2. Each State Party may at the time of signature or ratification of the present Convention or accession thereto declare that it does not consider itself bound by paragraph I of this article. The other States Parties shall not be bound by that paragraph with respect to any State Party which has made such a reservation.

3. Any State Party which has made a reservation in accordance with paragraph 2 of this article may at any time withdraw that reservation by notification to the Secretary-General of the United Nations.

Article 30
The present Convention, the Arabic, Chinese, English, French, Russian and Spanish texts of which are equally authentic, shall be deposited with the Secretary-General of the United Nations.

IN WITNESS WHEREOF the undersigned, duly authorized, have signed the present Convention.

www.ingramcontent.com/pod-product-compliance
Lightning Source LLC
Chambersburg PA
CBHW020601270326
41927CB00005B/125